Cover illustration:
Bather, 1900
(ornament for
a swimming-pool)

Translation:
Barbara Thompson

Design:
Sophie Bloch

Photogravure:
Kromosscan, Barcelone

Typography:
Acatène, Malakoff

Printed
February 1986
by Imprimerie Blanchard,
Le Plessis-Robinson

© Fernand Hazan,
Paris 1984

ISBN 2 85025 080 5

THE RODIN MUSEUM

text by monique laurent

photographs by bruno jarret

HAZAN

THE HÔTEL BIRON, THE RODIN MUSEUM.

Of the great houses in the rue de Varenne, described by eighteenth-century guide-books as "the most remarkable in the kingdom" the Hôtel Biron, the Rodin Museum since the first World War, with its stone walls, its greenery, its lawns and arbours suspended in time, seems to belong to a dream world, a world of delectation and happiness.

Its history dates back to 1728, when Abraham Peyrenc de Moras, a singular individual who might have stepped out of Lesage or Beaumarchais, grown rich by speculating on paper money and enjoying an international hearing, ordered the construction of "the most splendid house there was to be found in Paris". The plans attributed to Jacques Gabriel, then the Inspector of the King's Buildings, with whom the financier had carried out a number of transactions, were executed in two years by another famous architect, Jean Aubert. This comparatively brief space of time doubtless explains the homegeneity of the works.

Peyrenc died in 1731 and his widow let the house, barely fitted out, to the Duchess of Maine, the daughter-in-law of Louis XIV, who lived there until her death in 1753. The Peyrenc family then ceded the ownership to the Duke of Biron, a Marshal of France, whose name it was to bear henceforth. Biron was a hero of the wars of Louis XV, a renowned soldier fond of lavish display, who transformed the Hôtel into a rendezvous of fashion, where banquets and fêtes succeeded each other, including that given in 1782 in honour of the Grand Duke of Russia, the future Tsar, Paul 1.

Concerning that occasion the *Guide des amateurs et des étrangers visiteurs à Paris* (Guide for art-lovers and foreign visitors in Paris) records the exclamations of the guests at the wonders of the park adorned with "trellises forming porticoes, arcades, grottoes, domes, Chinese pavilions", for in those days, the gardens were the chief attraction of all great houses.

When the old Marshal died in 1788, the house fell to his nephew, the dashing and adventurous Duke of Lauzun, who had been the comrade-in-arms of La Fayette and Rochambeau in the Americain War of Independence, then a Commander in the Revolutionary Army on the Rhine and in Vendée, against the Chouans. He perished on the scaffold in 1793, despite the pledges given to the Jacobins.

Like most of the houses in the Faubourg Saint-Germain, the Hôtel Biron fell into disuse and its grounds were left to the devices of nature until 1797. Under the Directory, the Béthune-Charost family, the heirs of Lauzun, let the property to masters of public ceremonies, whose dances, concerts, fireworks, acrobatics, jugglers and even flying-balloons transformed its French gardens into a fairground.

The Consulate and the Empire, however, brought dwellers of a more solemn sort, the Hôtel being turned over first to the Papal Legation then to the Russian Embassy.

The elderly and devout Duchess of Charost, still its owner, expressed the dying wish that the house might be used for pious purposes and bequeathed it to the Company of the Sacred Heart of Jesus, formed in

1804 for the education of young ladies of the French and foreign aristocracy.

The founder, Mother Sophie Barat, threw her strength of character and her faith in Christian virtues into organizing a boarding-school which, owing to the excellence of the tuition dispensed and the high social rank of the pupils quickly gained prestige and prosperity. Its severe rule was designed to protect the boarders, among whom was Eugenia de Montijo, the future wife of Napoleon III, from the frivolities of the age, which was why Mother Sophie deemed it necessary to sell the interior fittings, the lintels painted by Lemoyne and Coypel, the framed glass reflecting the sumptuous white and gold panelling and the wrought iron-work. Long after she had taken up her abode, she deplored the fact that "unfortunately not all the finery had been removed".

Owing to the conflict over the separation of Church and State in 1904 the congregation was dissolved and the boarding-school closed. This ushered in a new period of uncertainty for the Hôtel.

The liquidator of the possessions of the religious community agreed that the abandoned buildings might be converted into temporary apartments while awaiting demolition and the parcelling out of the entire estate. These circumstances proved decisive for the safeguard of the house because the unusual charm and the surroundings of the makeshift apartments attracted many artists. Jean Cocteau recalled it in his *Portraits Souvenirs*, Matisse lived there, so did the actor De Max and, above all, urged on by the poet Rainer-Maria Rilke who was his secretary for a few months, Rodin. In 1908, Rodin was at the height of his international fame. Although his home was still the Villa des Brillants in Meudon where Rose Beuret lived and where his assistants worked, he went to the Hôtel Biron every day to entertain, to amass his personal collections and drawings and to stroll in the gardens where the old tracery was rapidly vanishing under the luxuriant vegetation left to run wild.

At last, in 1911, the house was bought by the State, the far end of the property being reserved for the Lycée Victor Duruy on the rue de Babylone ; but its ultimate fate remained to be settled.

The ensuing tergiversations brought forth a vast movement of opinion in favour of a museum devoted to Rodin. Statements and petitions from politicians and artists were signed by Monet, Octave Mirbeau, Poincaré, Clemenceau, Romain Rolland, Etienne Clémentel, but the project met with the hostility Rodin's work still aroused in certain influential circles and, in a more general way with the unwillingness of the State to grant one of its possessions to a living artist, however great. The First World War delayed matters until 1916, by which time Rodin had also made more concrete provisions for the destination of his works: by three successive donations, he bequeathed exclusively to the State the whole of his collections, his personal archives, his house in Meudon and, most important of all, the totality of his creative works, sculptures and drawings, with full reproduction rights. In 1919, the Hôtel Biron became the Auguste Rodin National Museum and opened its lofty gates to admit the public to one of the most poetic places in Paris. It has never closed them since.

The Thinker, 1906

The Walking Man, 1878

ENTRANCE HALL, AND VESTIBULE ROOM 1

The imperious stride of the *Walking Man* (1878, enlarged in 1907) dominates the Entrance Hall. his figure with neither arms nor head is thought to be a study for the *St. John the Baptist* (room 5). It breaks with academic tradition by ignoring the sacrosanct rule of the full representation of the human body and by bringing out the dynamics of the act of walking as the subject-matter of the work. The attitude suggests the sequence and permanence of the step, its gradual evolution, and introduces the notion of time passing, of duration, a theme which was to be taken up by the Futurists, especially by Boccioni in his studies of continuous movement in space.
As a prelude to the development of Rodin's art, nurtured on boldness but also on fidelity to the past, the small vestibule contains two traditional sculptures. The bust of his father, *Jean-Baptiste Rodin* (1860) with the bare shoulders treated in "the antique manner", the firm modelling and accurate contours, calls up the heroic nude advocated by neo-classical taste. The second piece, the *Vase with Titans* (1877 ?) in actual fact is a support for a garden ornament; it is surrounded by muscular figures in complex and anguished attitudes drawing largely on Michelangelo, supposedly sustaining a vase.
The sculpture bears the signature of Carrier-Belleuse, the fashionable sculptor and decorator of the Second Empire, in whose workshop Rodin was employed at the beginning of his career as an apprentice for the execution of decorative assignments based on the styles of the past.
The first room of the museum is devoted exclusively to the portraits carved from 1860-1870. These works illustrate Rodinś "conservative" phase to the extent that they reflect the different trends of earlier periods : realism, severe and slightly grimacing in the bust of the *Reverend Eymard*, the founder of the Order of the Very Blessed Sacrament which Rodin entered briefly after the death of his sister, Maria ; realism again, but impetuous and well-mastered, in the bust named *Mignon*, probably a portrait of Rose Beuret, Rodin's life-long companion, where the organization of the hair in loose unruly locks and the twist of the shoulders lend an almost baroque animation to the whole ; realism, once more, in the society portraits of *Mr. and Mrs. Garnier* ; realism, finally, in the bust of the *Man with the Broken Nose*, rejected in its terra-cotta version by the 1864 Salon. The veracity of this mutilated visage of an old man is underlined in a classical manner to achieve a more general interpretation of reality, depicting a type and not only a specific individual. It bears an obvious resemblance to the portraits of Greek philosophers Rodin studies in the Louvre. In contrast, a neo-rococo style echoing Carpeaux and even the eighteenth century finds expression in the profusion of ornaments bestowed on the *Girl in a flowered Hat*. Yet there is no feeling of pastiche ; on the contrary, the work is remarkable for its very personal fashioning, the unsophisticated volumes of the hair, the bold hollowing-out of the eyes and the velvety softness of the youthful skin.

Girl with a flowered Hat, 1865-1870

Young Woman and Child, 1865-1870

ROOM 2

The work shown here were executed between 1871 and 1877, the period when Rodin joined his employer, Carrier-Belleuse, in Brussels, as the outbreak of the Franco-Prussian War in 1870 had put a stop to all artistic activity in France. There, he carried out several important decorative assignments for public buildings, producing a type of allegorical sculpture in his work for the Stock Exchange, the Palais des Académies, the Royal School of Music and the facades of various apartment houses which recurs in some pleasing and gracefully alive figures such as the *Bacchante*, the *Spring* or the *Young Woman and Child*. It should be noted in passing that the theme of motherhood is common to the most academic artists. During the period of economic anxiety that Rodin clearly conformed to public taste, although he endowed his subjects with an elegance and freedom betraying the sensuality that always stirred his imagination.

The theme of children or cherubs was also part of the ornamental repertoire of the day. It appears here in the *Children with a Lizard* and the *Idyll at Ixelles* where the chubby forms, the soft flesh and the still uncertain features combine a reminiscence of eighteenth-century cupids and the more realistic image of Auguste, the son of Rodin and Rose Beuret, born in 1866, who had stayed in France.

Other works belonging to the difficult years include imaginary subjects like the bust of *Suzon* or *Dosia*, idealized portraits of girls with a purely decorative function, typical examples of the rather insipid art bronzes that were widely disseminated among a middle-class clientèle by numerous dealers. But Rodin was also busy with real portraiture. He took his friends as his models, the Belgian sculptor, *Paul de Vigne*, whose expressive bust is a visible likeness and in sharp contrast to the conventional realism of that of *Alexandre Van Beckelaer*, the apothecary who assisted Rodin financially, as he wrote to Rose : "I have no money at all for the time being ; luckily a chemist and one of my friends have helped me out ; otherwise I do not know what I should have done".

The *Girl with Flowers in her Hair* allies the discreet naturalism of a face carved with clear-cut and firm volumes and the brio of the garland adorning her hair. Works like this illustrate Rodin's technical virtuosity which is one of the reasons accounting for the scope of his creative activity. Being obliged to undertake so much decorative work, Rodin had become familiar with almost every aspect of sculpture and may indeed be the last of the great sculptors to have had such ja manysided training.

The "Belgian period" also provided him with an opportunity to improve his artistic education by observing old masters and to try out his hand at other techniques. The "squared" study after Ruben's *Descent from the Cross* in Antwerp cathedral, the large studies of male nudes, true nudes in the most academic sense of the word, and the landscapes of the surroundings of Brussels in the manner of some pre-impressionist painters bear witness to this.

Above:
Brother and Sister, 1890
and Young Mother, 1885
▶

Above: Fugit Amor, 1885. Below: Mother and Child, 1866-1870

Below: Children with a Lezard, towards 1886 and the Bacchante, 1876

The Age of Bronze, 1876

ROOM 3

The Oval Drawing-Room or Large East Study was one of the state rooms of the Hôtel Biron. The original fittings, among the most brilliant of the eighteenth century, were retored about fifteen years ago. The chief feature of this room is the radiant figure of the *Age of Bronze*, conceived by Rodin after a jouney to Italy in the winter of 1875. Rodin's intent analysis of Michelangelo's technique, striving to dismantle the works in order to understand the mechanisms, carving by planes, mobility of muscles, dynamic unity as opposed to the stability of classical Greek sculpture is summed up in the *Age of Bronze*, the first life-size statue in which Rodin achieved a synthesis betwen the study from nature and the influence of the Italian Renaissance. Shown in 1877, it brought forth the insulting accusation that it had been cast directly on the model's body, as the authenticity of the anatomy contrasted startlingly with the cold "nudes" to which the public was accustomed. The ensuing scandal at east had the merit of attracting attention to Rodin who was about to return to France to fulfil his ambitions.

To do so, he had to tackle several types of sculpture and first and foremost that required for public monuments. Rodin duly entered the *Call to Arms* in the competition organized in 1879 for a statue to commemorate the defence of Paris during the 1870 war. It was a group consisting of a dying warrior whose limp attitude recalled that of the dead Christ in Michelangelo's *Pietà* in the cathedral in Florence, and a fighting genuis wearing a Phrygian cap who, with his furious demeanour and savage cry derived from Rude's *Marseillaise* on the Arc de Triomphe in Paris. It was not the accuracy of the references that caused the project to be rejected but general reasons concerning the spirit of the work, considered too vibrant, too restless, too fierce.

During the last quarter of the nineteenth century the use of the human face gradually became widespread owing to the development of photography. At that time, Rodin began his portraits of renowned personalities : the bust of Carrier-Belleuse, carved in 1881 towards the end of their association, is a kind of tribute in the shape of a sensitive and brilliant rendering where the movement, the dishevelled hair and the skilful carelessness of the detailed dress recalls the vigour of eighteenth-centutry portraits of artists. The bust of *Dalou* (1883), one of the great official artists of the Third Republic, on the contrary is treated in broad planes, with no concessions to detail, austerely portraying the combative spirit and the nervous temperament of the model.

The common theme of Rodin's women's portraits is that the models counted in his social and emotional life. *Rose Beuret in Alsatian dress* is an unusual view of his devoted and jealous companion, in the guise of the province lost in 1870. Little is known of *Mrs A.D.* but her portrait aroused comment when shown at the Salon of 1879 on account of its meticulous yet firm handling, its candid naturalism and its plastic authority heralding the great works of the next decade.

The Call to Arms, 1877-1879

Room 4. Foreground, the Eternal Idol, 1889

ROOM 4

In the centre of this drawing-room, the former anteroom of the officers of the Duchess of Maine, stands the *Hand of God* (1898), an ambitious work both in size and symbolical meaning. With this portrayal of the birth of man and woman, Rodin appeals directly to the imagination, establishing a relationship between the clay moulded by the divine hand and the creativity of the artist modelling formless matter. From what we know of Rodin's artistic sources, the choice of representing divinity solely by a hand was probably guided by the medieval and Renaissance tradition which frequently shows God as a hand emerging from the clouds. Rodin used the hand belonging to one of the figures of the *Burghers of Calais*, transforming the gesture of despair of the hostage awaiting sacrifice into dynamic action (see room 11). This ability to alter the signifiance of a form radically by endowing it with a different and often totally opposite interpretation is a familiar component of Rodin's plastic idiom. Assembled round the pair brought into being between the marble fingers are related groups. For Rodin, the portrayal of lovers was an inexhaustible theme which allowed him to express every shade of passion, tenderness and sensuality. *Eternal Spring* (1884) belongs to the cycle of the *Kiss*, shown in the next room. The success of this group, also called *Zephyr and the Earth, Youth, the Ideal*, was so great that countless versions were made in bronze, popularizing its forms infused with youthful impetuosity and lyricism. The same splendid female torso, arched and rapturous, is found in the group entitled *Illusions received by the Earth*, personifying the vanity of dreams doomed to return to the soil. In the *Eternal Idol*, also called the *Host*, Rodin explored the relationship between man and woman in an even more complex fashion ; the captivating simplicity of this triangular composition is at once a celebration of a woman's beauty by her male partner and an expression of the all-powerful indifference of the *femme fatale* "surveying as if from a quiet hill-top the man beneath her". (R.M. Rilke). It should be noted that the allusions in the titles and their potential meanings reveal Rodin's close acquaintance with symbolist poetry. Two women's portraits also command attention : first, the marble bust, perhaps carved by Bourdelle, showing the faithful *Rose Beuret*, quiet, serious, almost stern then, on the chimney-piece, the bust of *Mrs. de Morla-Vicuna* (1884), the wife of a Chilean diplomat in Paris. Rodin rendered her beauty in full volumes over which the light plays gently, maintaining a discreet reserve in respect of his model. Recalling his portraits of women, he explained "even there, always the truth but not all the truth. Sometimes we must let the veil drop just a little". The interest of this work is further enhanced by the carefully detailed ornamentation of the blouse, almost contrasting with the peaceful expression of the face, distributed asymmetrically to soften the base of the bust in the manner of Carpeaux.

The Illusions received by the Earth, towards 1895

The Eternal Spring, 1884

The Eternal Idol, 1889

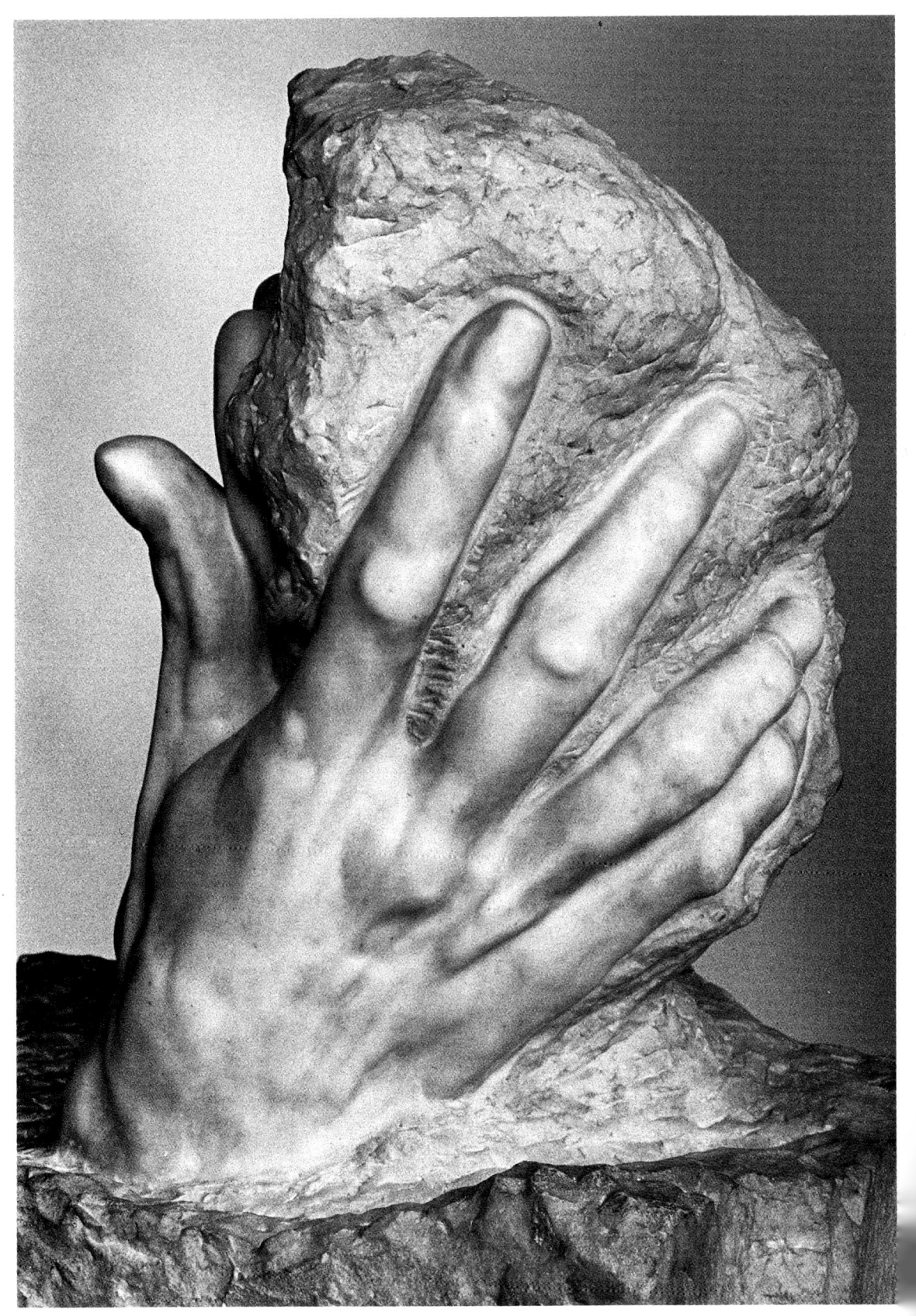

The Hand of God, 1898

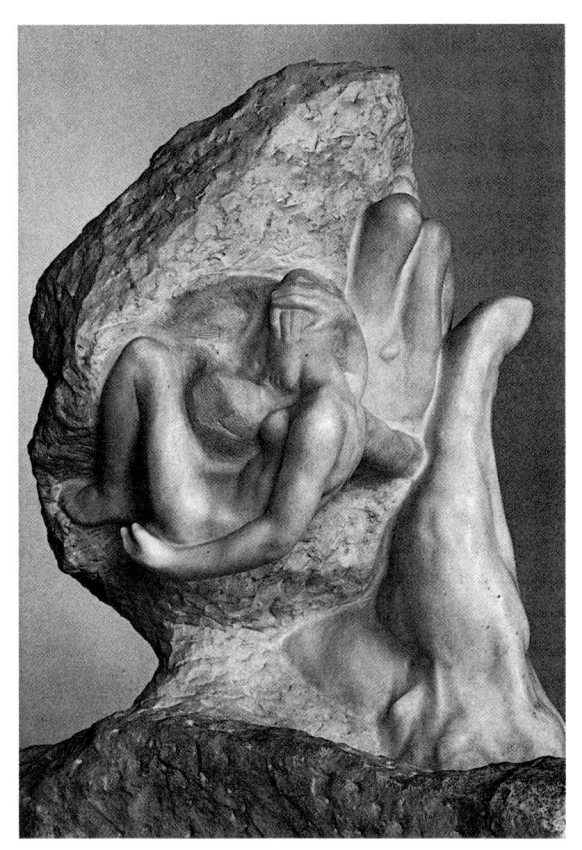

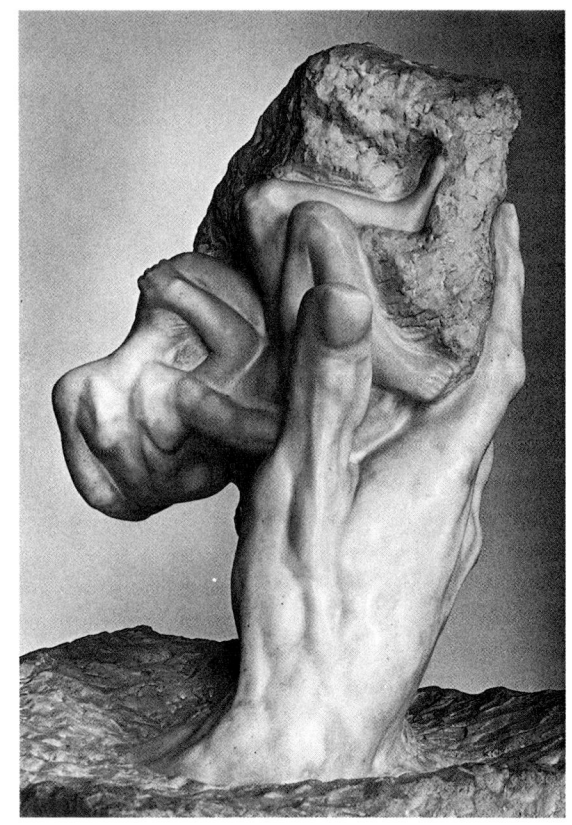

Room 5, general view

ROOM 5

The Large Central Drawing-room, also designed for receptions, separates the two large ground-floor apartments looking on to the garden. Formerly the walls were decorated with pilasters carved in varnished oak and with tall mirrors in gilded frames. The chimney-piece was in Flemish marble and painted allegories of the four parts of the day adorned the lintels of the doors.

The outstanding pieces assembled here may be regarded almost as a series of variations on the theme of the human body, from which Rodin drew all manner of emotional effects. The *St. John the Baptist* (1878) marks a definite break with academic sculpture by the fundamental innovation in the simulation of movement achieved by "the two legs open like a compass".. Using a highly conventional subject, Rodin introduced a new physical type, nervous and muscular, less spiritual and more robust than in customary iconography, giving energy to the demonstrative gesture, the parted lips, the hallucinated eyes. The visitor will notice the likeness to the model for the neo-antique *Torso* of the *Walking Man*.. Rodin had kept a plaster copy of this work, showing the traces of the tools and notches and had it cast in that state, aware that the sight of the stigmata preserved in the bronze would heighten the violence and emotion of the work.

Beside such vehemence, the *Kiss* (1886) displays the skilful entwining of rounded forms, totally closed in on themselves. This rendering of the guilty passion of Paolo Malatesta for his sister-in-law, Francesca da Rimini, can hardly be claimed as the most audacious of Rodin's portrayals of lovers yet it has always been looked upon as a symbol of erotic art.

Energy and dynamism define *Iris, Messenger of the Gods*, whose profiled silhouette seems to float in space, the body offered up, its flight arrested by carved form. Primacy is given to the onward thrust, the striking posture, and action; the idle parts of the body, no longer essential, having been discarded according to principale of elimination. Rodin simplified anatomy as long as it remained intelligible and conveyed meaning, sometimes arriving at highly stylized synthetic volumes and contours as in the headless *Torso* seen from the back (1913), polished like a pebble, like a Brancusi.

In other cases, like the *Prayer*, the frontal portrayal and the frank carving of the limbs accentuate the allegiance to classical sculpture, despite the powerful simplification suggesting certain nudes by Maillol. Rodin therefore approached the human body with methods that were very new for his time, fragmentation but also multiplication, consisting in grouping identical forms and engendering new and complex rhythms between surface planes and hollows. The *Cathedral* is one of the most subtle examples; it is composed of two right hands and yet our visual conditioning is such that they seem hard to identify although the mystifying effect is the outcome of a harmonious process cleverly preventing the same fingers from touching. In spite of the title due to the shape of the raised hands recalling a Gothic arch, the work was intended to decorate a fountain.

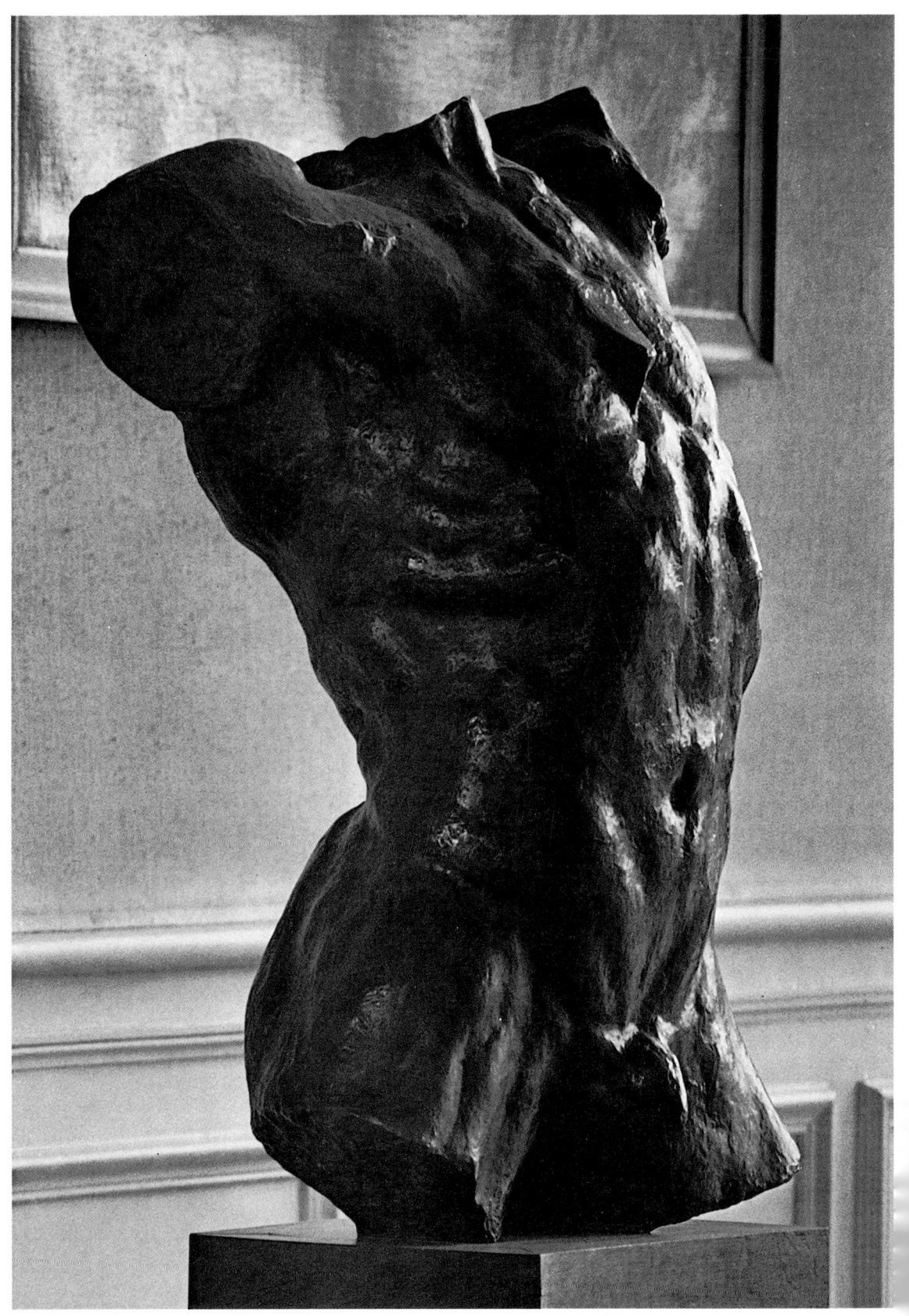
Torso, 1882

The Prayer, 1909

The Kiss, 1886

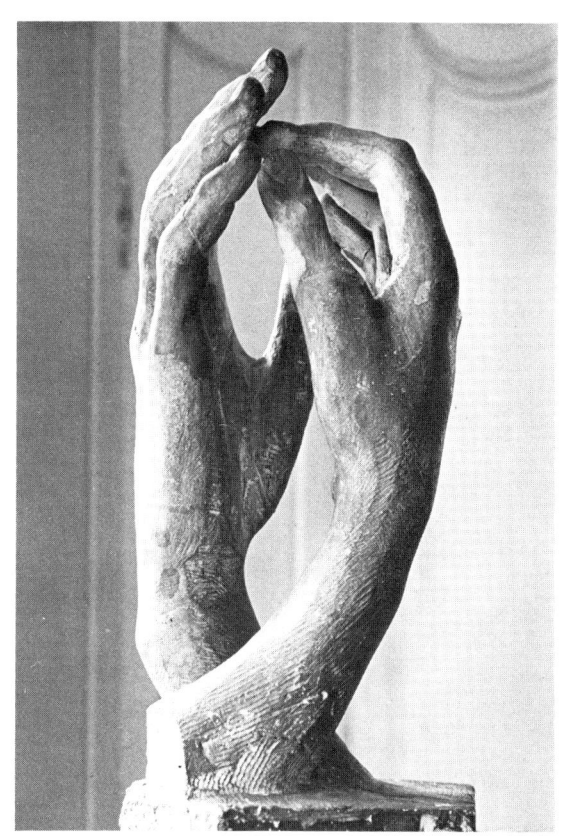

The Cathedral, 1908

Dawn, 1885

ROOM 6

This fine drawing-room, with partially reconstructed panelling was likewise used as a reception room by the Duchess of Maine. It now houses the two sculptures inspired by Camille Claudel (1864-1943) and a number of her own works. Camille Claudel was Rodin's student, model, assistant and mistress, until she succumbed to the excesses and extreme dejection of madness.

Thought (1886-89) by Rodin, is the most striking of these works owing to the contrast between the delicate and grave melancholy of Camille's untroubled face and the rough marble cube from which it emerges. This very symbolist conception of the opposition of mind and matter is also felt in the other renderings of the features of the "glorious girl", as her brother Paul called her: *Dawn*, bringing forth from the marble an "impressive air of courage, frankness, superiority, gaiety" (Paul Claudel); and *Farewell*, carved in 1892, a reference to the first break between the couple. In counterpoint, Camille's sculpture shares the lyrical tremor of Rodin's art but also fiercely asserts its independence. *Vertumnus and Pomona*, often compared to the *Eternal Idol* and the *Kiss* takes on an extra shade of ardent chastity and of perfectly balanced sensibility going beyond its impassioned character. Just as personal, the *Waltz* (1891-1905) does not depict the worldly grace of ballroom-dancers but by a skilful imbalance in the couple whirling in space imparts an elation doubtless largely autobiographical.

Camille Claudel again displays her independent genius and her technical skill in the group of *Chattering Women* (1898-1905) in onyx, a material rarely used and not yielding readily to the chisel, which heightens its *fin-de-siècle* strangeness. The complex lines of these four tiny figures with their crossed arms and curved backs were inspired by the sight of young women exchanging confidences in a narrow railway compartment. By choosing to miniaturize an everyday subject Camille Claudel again clearly set herself apart from Rodin. She was also a portraitist who strove for more than an objective likeness. The Swiss critic, Mathias Morhardt, described the portrait she modelled of Rodin in 1888 as a harsh work: "distinguished by the fact that from whatever angle it is viewed, the profiles are always accurate, there are no weaknesses, no afterthoughts, no doubts (.....). It is a patient and thorough work (...). And it is dramatic: it is presented majestically like a granite construction of ancient times". In the portrait of *Jeanne as a Child*, a girl encountered near Azay-le-Rideau where Camille Claudel had accompanied Rodin in his quest for preparatory documents for the *Balzac*, or to hide a pregnancy which was to miscarry, the expression is so intense, lucid and fervent, almost inspired, that it has been thought to portray Joan of Arc. Such was not Camille's intention but the plastic strength of the youthful features brings the association to mind.

Chattering Women, by C. Claudel, 1895

Vertumnus and Pomona, by C. Claudel, 1888

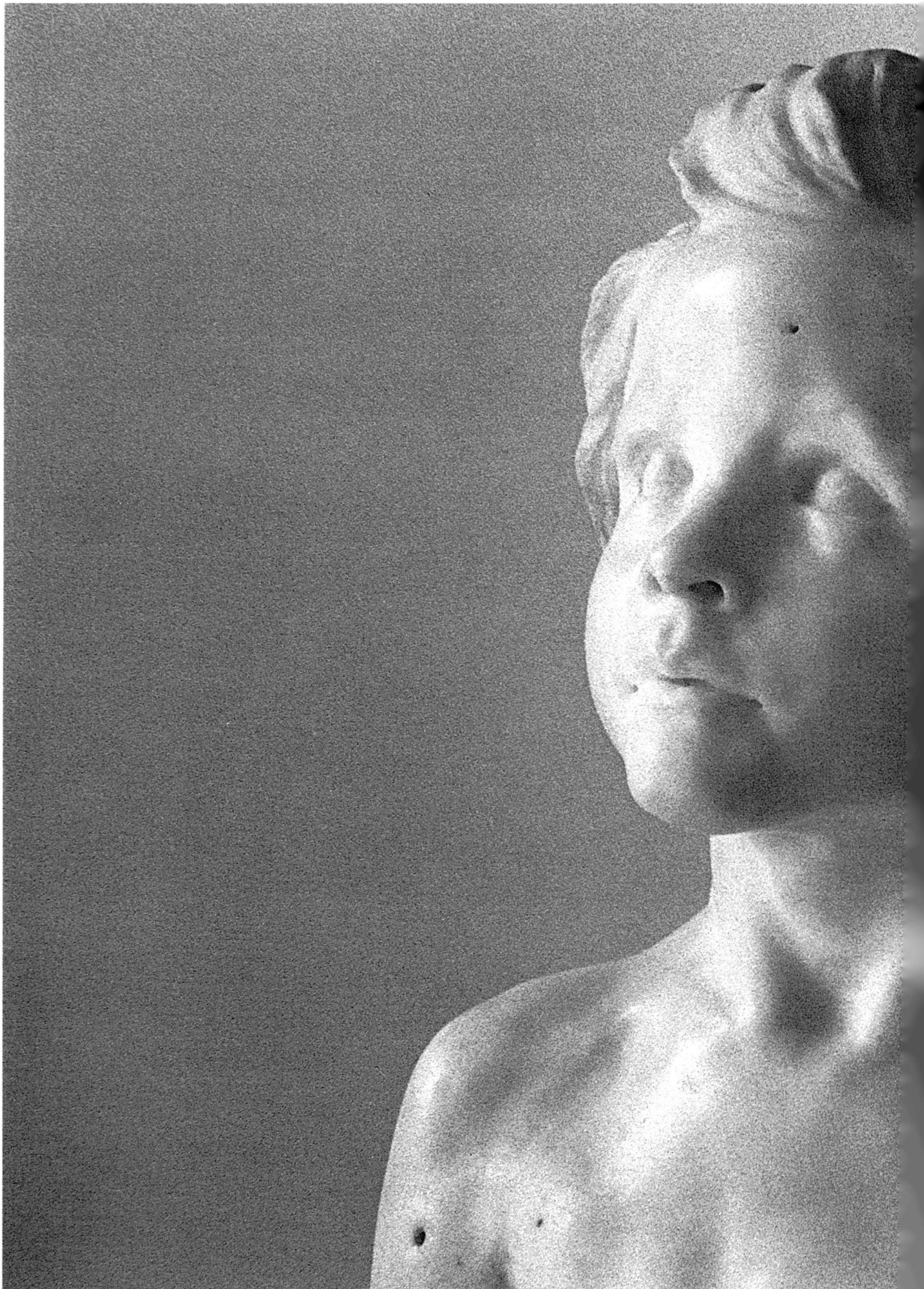

Jeanne as a child, by C. Claudel, 1894

Eve, 1881

ROOM 7

The panelling in this room, called the Large West Study or Oval Drawing-Room is characterized by its fluid style, a fondness for asymmetry and movement particularly remarkable in the magnificent frames of the mirrors in the shape of palm-leaves. They are attributed to the decorator, Nicolas Pineau, who worked at Versailles and several royal castles as well as Peterhof, the residence of Peter the Great near Leningrad.

The chief figure is the great bronze *Eve*, Rodin's first life-size carving of a female nude. Like a large *Adam* very close to that of Michelangelo, it was designed to frame the *Gates of Hell* (see Gardens). Adam and Eve was a very popular subject among academic sculptors, who drew on its sensuality (one has only to think of the enormous success of the *New Eve* by Paul Dubois at the 1873 Salon, the *Eve after the Fault*, by Alfred Boucher in 1875 or the *Eve* by Marqueste in 1888. Rodin seems to have respected a certain Salon manner in his treatment here and tempered the references to Renaissance art, which inspired his *Adam*. Rumour has it that while he was working as usual from a live model, he discovered that she was expecting a child and so found himself constantly obliged to alter the volumes and contours of the work until he had to leave it partly unfinished. The surface of certain parts of the body, the abdomen in particular, indeed seem rougher, less polished than in other sculptures from the same period. The heel prop which helped the model to keep her leg bent without fatigue has even been kept in the bronze to counterbalance the figure. This choice, like the decision to keep the "seams" or network of lines in relief corresponding to the plan joining the different parts of the mould of the plaster model needed for the cast, bears witness to Rodin's eagerness to respect the technical realities of his craft and bring them to the public's notice.

Round the *Eve*, several groups of figures often drawn from Greek mythology illustrate subjects which Rodin hoped would people the *Gates of Hell* and express allegorically the anguish of the soul (see rooms 9 and 10 and gardens). The fabled *Centauress*, half human and half beast, symbolizes the duality of instinct and intellect; the *Siren-Meditation* and the *Siren-Toilet of Venus*, changed into fantastic creatures, are variations on the female anatomies of the lintel; the same burgeoning sensuality is found in the group of *Orpheus and the Maenads*, where Orpheus, as an androgyne, bereft of Eurydice, grapples with the consorts of Dionysus in prey to sacred delirium. The somewhat chill serenity of the marble bust on the chimney-piece constrasts with the spell of these provocative forms. It was inspired by the perfect purity of the features of Marianne Russell, the wife of the Australian painter, John Russell; its wholly classical conception, with the shoulders covered in flowing drapery, suggest that Rodin wished to pay a kind of tribute to antique sculpture with a portrayal of the goddess Minerva.

Room 8, general view

ROOM 8

Room 8 is entirely devoted to portraits of women executed after 1900, the date of the vast display of 170 sculptures in the context of the Exposition Universelle. It was against the background of an absorbing social life, official duties unsolicited but readily taken up, the direction of a large workshop and more and more admirers daily that these portraits were carved for the high fees Rodin then asked as a mark of his fame. The variety of sizes, compositions, materials — bronze, marble, terra-cotta, plaster — is amazing in such conventional work. Each of the busts asserts its identity, the resemblance lying above all in the expression of individual character. The severe and sensitive face of the beautiful Englishwoman, *Eve Fairfax*, imparts her energy by the frontal presentation; *Lady Sackville West*, on the contrary, is shown as if asleep, her head resting sideways on a marble block deliberately left rough to set off the fluidity of the facial features. The same dreamy expression, the same complexity in the contours, but enhanced by the application of discreet polychrome characterizes the bust of *Mrs. Fenaille*, the wife of Rodin's faithful and efficient friend who, after helping him in his career, became one of the administrators of the museum making generous donations. Never before, perhaps, had the psychological reading of a model attained the poetic quality of this "portrait of soul". It stands in rather cruel contrast to that of the redoutable *Duchess of Choiseul*; from 1905 to 1911 for Rodin she was a provocative and shrewd Egeria, who isolated him from his old friends, luring him into the adulterated world of scheming and intrigue. The image he gives of her here seems like an unpitying moral testimony where the vivacious smile and the false gaiety of the eyes fail to dissimulate the grasping personality.

The friendship and reciprocal admiration shared by Carrière and Rodin are well-known. An illustration of their convergent ideals will be found by associating Carrière's *Motherhood* and the *Mother and dying child* carved by Rodin in 1905 for the tomb of the daughter of Mrs. Thomas Merrill: the maternal feelings are expressed with the same pictorial and plastic effects, all sentimentality removed, the entire concern being to convey a poignant and dignified portrayal of "inner clarity".

English and American customers were not the only ones to seek out Rodin. This is attested by other portraits, such as that of *Mrs. de Goloubeff*, the Caucasian, one of the muses and translators of Gabriele d'Annunzio, and the beautiful *Mrs. Elissieff*, whose bust in marble was carved by Despiau under Rodin's supervision and is now kept in the Hermitage Museum in Leningrad.

The Slavonic Woman, displaying the consistency and the smooth volumes of her portly shoulders and her highly personal looks occupies the centre of the room. This bust was recently identified as the Czech artist, Braunerova, a renowned painter and engraver and the sister-in-law of the symbolist novelist, Elemir Bourges.

43

DRAWINGS ROOM

Few visitors are aware of the existence of the collection of graphics boasting about seven thousand items, which Rodin left to the State along with his sculptures. Since 1981, owing to the number, the drawings have been exhibited by a three-monthly rota system in accordance with conservation norms. Although the themes are the same as those of the sculptures and display a feeling for volume typical of the sculptor's craft, Rodin regarded drawing as a creative activity totally separate from his three-dimensional research. By paying random visits, the public will therefore be able to discover early copies of old masters, gouaches and brown washes inspired by the great literary works of all periods, Ovid's *Metamorphoses*, Dante's *Inferno*, Baudelaire's *Fleurs du Mal* — and, above all, the countless sketches fixing the female body in the most varied attitudes with bold uncluttered lines, enhanced in water-colour.

Above: Cambodian dancing girl.
Below: Illustration of the *Jardin des Supplices*

Above: Dance movement and Draped crouching Woman
Below: Seated female nude and Cambodian dancing girl

Staircase, first landing, the three Shades, 1880

STAIRCASE

Three major works await the visitor mounting the grand staircase. On the first landing, the group of the *Three Shades* crowning the *Gates of Hell* personifies the shades described by Dante in Canto XVI of the *Inferno*. Their bowed and tortuous stance, as if weighed down with grief, seems to provide a visual equivalent of the famous sentence: "Abandon all hope, ye who enter here". The *Three Shades* seems almost a deliberate illustration of Rodin's "profile" method. This consisted first and foremost in fixing the general outline of a sculpture, "contrasting the curves and the planes" so as to determine the volume and obtain a living shape. In these strictly identical figures viewed respectively from the left, the front and the right, there are no repetitions of contours, no symmetry effects; the interest lies in the group as a whole, it is not dependent on a few strong points. Yet the variety of the animated profiles delineating the sculpture in space does not entirely account for the use of figures which are alike; repetitive grouping was one of Rodin's boldest inventions but he never explained why he chose it. We can do more than note the result: new rhythms more complex and more dynamic, adding to the overall impact. Once again, duplication serves to suggest duration, the evolution of a single form in time. There has been much speculation on the meaning of the mutilation suppressing the right hand of the *Three Shades*. By depriving the figures of their creative hand, their working hand, Rodin seems to have wished to suggest man's powerlessness in the face of destiny and the fruitlessness of all endeavour before the ineluctable.

At the corner of the second landing stands the grim *Bellone*. In 1879, Rodin entered this sculpture in a competition designed to choose a bust of the Republic for municipal buildings in Paris. It was not selected, on the grounds that its violent and dramatic character, accentuated by the magnificent warrior's helmet, likened it more to the goddess of war than the Republic which, in the political context of the day, had to be portrayed as serene and reassuring. It was too compelling, too expressive, too remote from the tradition. The model for the bust was doubtless Rose Beuret but the pronounced almost virile features show that Rodin did not set out to portray her character realistically. Finally, on the upper floor, the convulsed body of the *Martyr* is again a figure taken from the *Gates of hell*. Viewed in isolation, it has sometimes been called the *Christian Martyr* although it seems closer to an interpretation of sensual passion, a sign of the tendency to identify love with suffering so frequent in Rodin. Visually, the work contains a new and striking idea which also interested Degas, that of suppressing the base to allow the sculpture to rest directly on the stand. The voluptuous forms and the expressive torsion of the limbs were used and adapted by Rodin in other pieces (The *Fall of Icarus*) offering a typical example of creative work by a variety of combinations and ramifications.

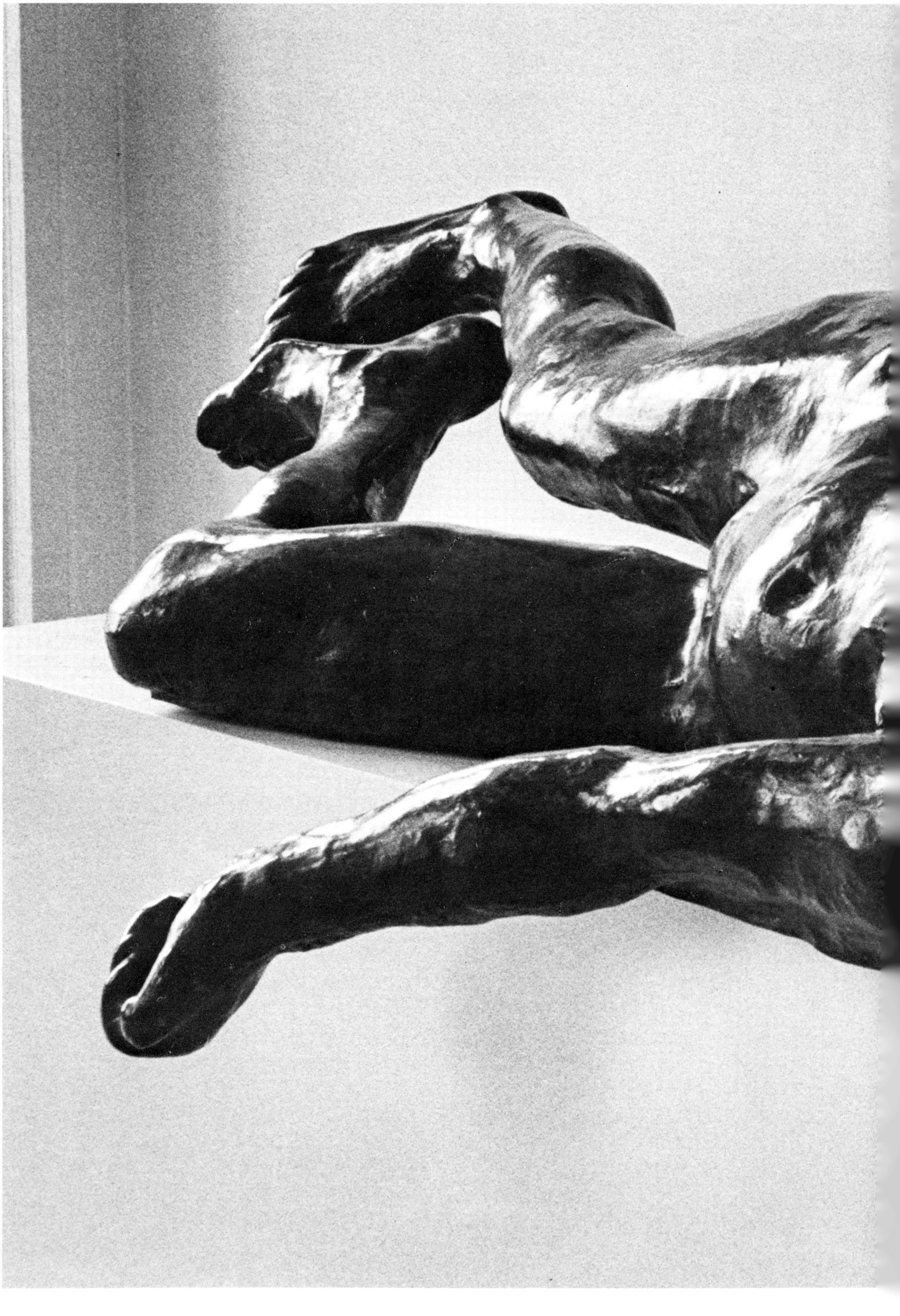

The Martyr, 1885

Room 9, general view

ROOM 9

This room is devoted to the studies for the *Gates of Hell*.
In 1880 Rodin was commissioned to compose a work on a grand scale which would serve as the triumphal entrance to the new Museum of Decorative Arts. The work never reached its initial destination and the many figures Rodin devised to cover its doors were exhibited separately. In other words, the *Gates of Hell* became a breeding and training ground for an artist eager to try out his plastic inventions, an opportunity to extol the human body. Rodin made use of the expressive qualities of the nude without the slightest hypocrisy unlike the majority of sculptors in his day who disguised them beneath a veil of prettiness.

The theme of the *Gates* is based on Part One of Dante's *Divine Comedy*. Rodin did not seek to give a literal illustration of the poem or its symbolical and allegorical structure, he chose to bring out its pathos, its violence, its dramatic potentialities and, so doing, represented the passions, conflicts and sorrows colouring his own life.

The Thinker is shown here in the original size, as he appears in the centre of the *Gates*. Identified in turn as Minos, the judger of souls, Dante the poet or Rodin himself contemplating his creation, the *Thinker* rapidly acquired a more general meaning pertaining to man's intellectual powers. A painting by Edvard Munch representing this sculpture in the garden of a German collector was purchased by the Rodin Museum in 1981, the first canvas by the Norwegian expressionist painter to enter a French public collection. Each character designed for the *Gates* possesses its own particular strength. The *Prodigal Son* is an image of despair, imposed directly and concisely without anecdotal references to the parable. "I sharpened the projection of the muscles to convey distress, I exaggerated the span of the tendons to indicate the yearning of prayer." (Rodin, *Art*, conversations collected by Paul Gsell). The same feelings are embodied in the *Despair* but this time by a curved female figure, bending inwards, perhaps inspired by the exercizes of dancers.

Various studies bear witness to the gestation of this vast composition. On the right in the exhibition case two wax models show the very first thoughts : initially just a geometrical outline, then a tiny model with drops of wax kneaded with the finger already indicating characters and groups. There are also a few plaster casts of some of the major figures : the *Kneeling Fauness* with its scared features, where sensual passion is rendered by an attitude expressing the awareness of physical beauty ; the *Torso of Adèle* deploying its independent form unrelated to any specific project ; the *Man Falling*, his fine physique recalling the steady influence of the work of Michelangelo on Rodin in the eighties. The group of *Three Faunesses* is a new example of repetitive composition with three identical figures. They support one another to form a round, the right and left foot touching the ground alternately to mark the beat. This piece conjures up Maenads in ritual play or ecstasy leading back to the obsessive idea of pagan eroticism in Rodin.

Studies for the Gates of Hell, 188

Studies for the Gates of Hell

Crouching Woman, 1882

ROOM 10

More subjects from the *Gates of Hell* are shown in this room, works which Rodin endowed with a life of their own by casting them in bronze or carving them in marble. The nervous and sophisticated handling of the *Danaïd* obliges the spectator to move round it because there is no angle from which the splendid prostrate figure can be viewed fully. The group *Fugit Amor*, also in marble, is presumed to illustrate the adulterous damned who are tormented by an infernal wind in the second circle of Hell. This couple indeed seems propelled by an invisible force and the figures joined back to back at once clutch and strain away from each other as if caught in an everlasting race to the abyss. The *Crouching Woman*, placed on the right of the *Thinker* in the *Gates*, is a bold figure in a complex attitude which may have been inspired by Michelangelo's *Crouching Youth*. This posture raised the problem of the join between the knee and the right cheek. The contrast between the undulating surfaces of the brow and the left cheek and the angular facets of the right cheek display Rodin's scorn of the "conventional" finish so prized by academic sculpture. By combining this figure with the *Falling Man* (see room 9) Rodin created a new work called "I am beautiful", in reference to Baudelaire's lines carved on the base. Rodin had used a drawing of this sculpture to illustrate a poem from the *Fleurs du Mal* and the relationships of the assemblage bear witness to the ingenious functioning of his imagination in respect of Baudelaire's universe.

Another poem, by François Villon, inspired the title of the *Old Courtesan*, "she who was the beautiful helmet-maker's wife", a startlingly realistic portrait of the decrepitude of old age. Reconsidering his approach to beauty and ugliness, discarding the references to Michelangelo, Rodin drew closer to naturalism and was more faithful to anatomical peculiariaties in his treatment of this subject. He explained why in his conversations with Paul Gsell : "only strength of character makes for beauty in art and it often happens that the uglier a person is in nature, the more beautiful that person is in art.... What is ugly in art is what is false, what is artificial, what tries to be pretty or lovely instead of being expressive."

This definition of truthful expression the first criterion is demonstrated in an impressive way in the group of *Ugolino* and his children. The theme, often portrayed in the nineteenth century, illustrates the punishment of Count Ugolino, the tyrant of Pisa, condemned to die of hunger after devouring the corpses of his children who were imprisoned with him. Adopting a construction of curved lines closing the forms in on themselves, Rodin made Ugolino into a kind of reptile surrounded by his dying offspring. The quasi-abolition of conscious mind becomes particularly plain in the careful modelling of the half-crazed face ; at the same time the youthful and vigorous body is detailed as if to stress its inhuman vitality.

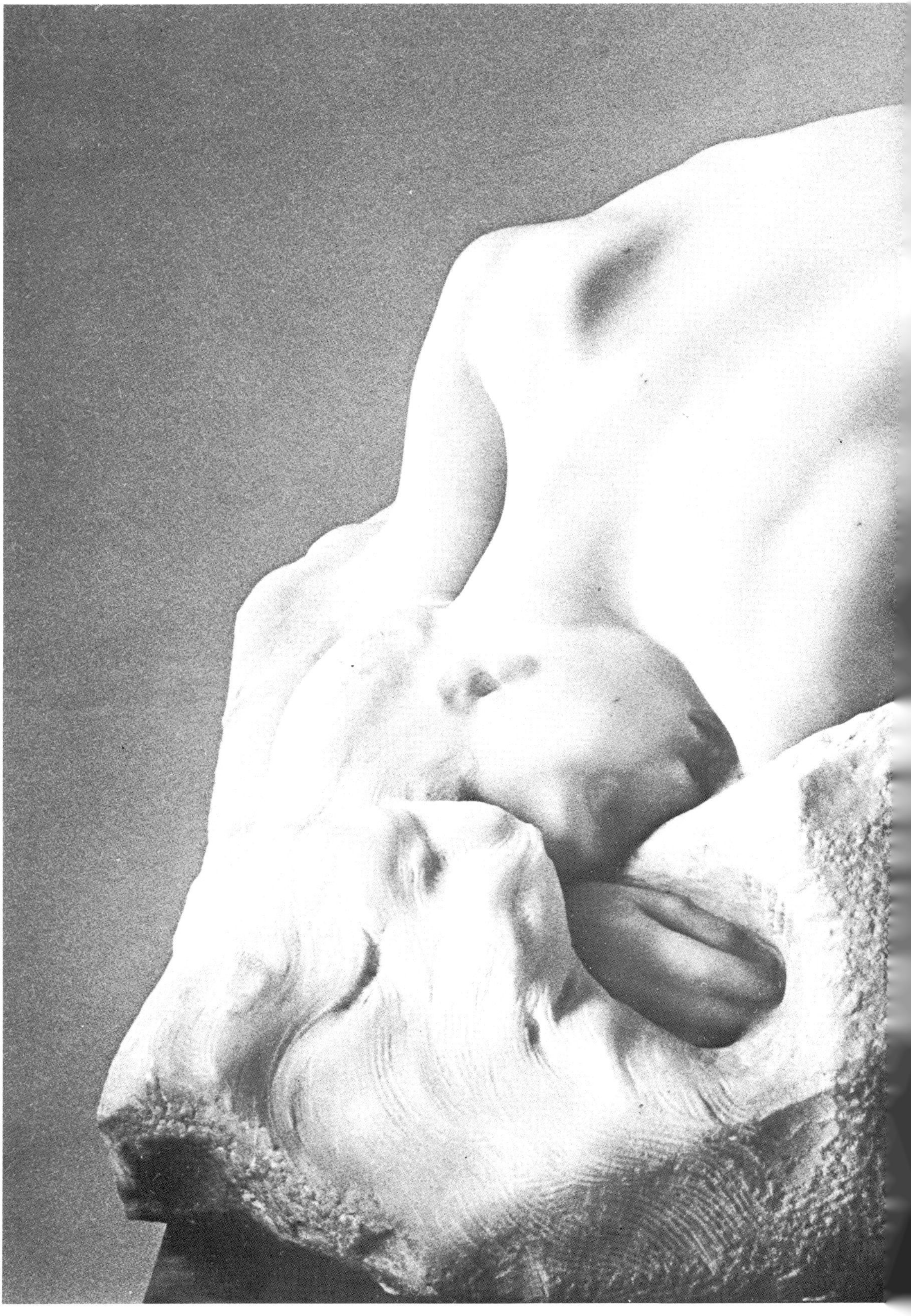

Danaïd, 1885

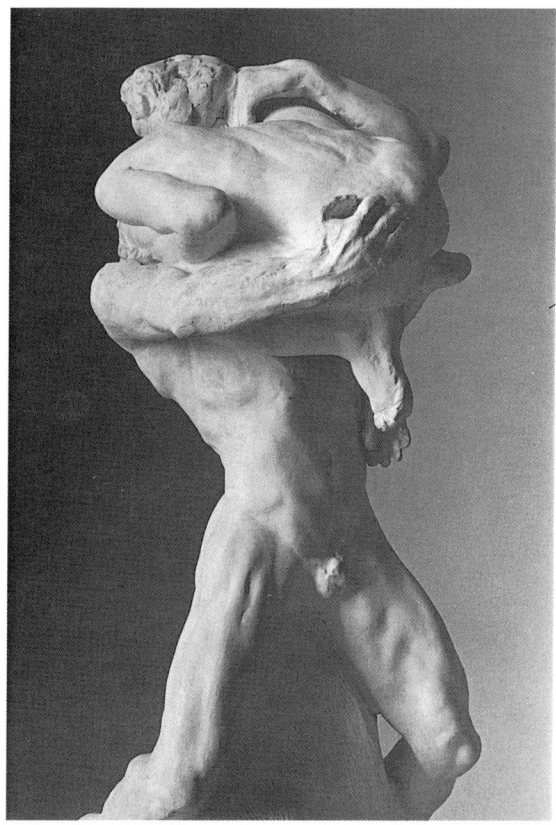

I am Beautiful, 1882

Caryatid with a stone, before 1881

Second model for the Burghers of Calais, 1886

ROOM 11

Here are the most significant pieces relating to the *Burghers of Calais*, one of Rodin's major achievements. This work was commissioned in 1884 by the city of Calais to recall the famous episode of the Hundred Years War recounted in the Chronicles of Froissart. The city, besieged by Edward III of England, was spared in exchange for the sacrifice of six of its notables, portrayed here as hostages dressed in long shirts, barefoot and with a rope round their necks ready to be hanged. They were saved only by the intercession of Queen Philippa of Hainaut.

Tradition advocated a pyramidal structure dominated by a glorified hero, with pompous allegories. Far from respecting that tradition, Rodin broke with the convention altogether by adopting a group of six figures which, instead of praising a single man, introduced an idea of collectively consented sacrifice. This schema is evolved in the first model (exhibition case) in the shape of a cube, assembling a life-like and coherent group on a triumphal pedestal. It is followed by a second model studying the personal approach to death of each of the protagonists. Filled with determination, resignation, anxiety or despair, the Burghers, wearing the homespun of condemned men, seem to be proceeding slowly forwards. The anatomy is clearly perceptible beneath the garments because the nudes were constructed beforehand. This becomes plain from a comparison with the various studies carved from the models who walked freely about his workshop. Rodin paid special attention to the faces as was his wont and the outcome is a series of very highly individualized carvings. He saw Eustache de Saint-Pierre as an emaciated elder with flaccid skin and a far-away look in his eyes as if already apprehending death; Jean d'Aire, the bearer of the keys of the city, on the contrary conveys an energy rendered visually by the well-shaped round head and the set lips; the pathos of the head of Pierre de Wissant springs from the dissymmetrical fashioning and the wrinkled and pitted features catching the light. The oversize enlargement of this head, which was shown for the first time in 1909, is remarkable as an example of the influence of colossal Hellenistic sculpture on Rodin at that time Using the procedure he had adopted for the heads and the nudes, Rodin made separate studies of some of the hands. This enabled him to heighten the personalities of the protagonists by prolonging and dramatizing their movements.

A few assemblages complete the display. These are hybrid works which illustrate the full complexity of Rodin's creative approach. They are made up of fragments relating to the *Burghers of Calais* – heads or hands – combined with foreign elements such as a female torso or a woman's face. The method of producing a work of art by means of pre-existing pieces was to become an important feaure of twentieth-century sculpture where the assembly technique was applied either to parts of sculptures or to manufactured objects deviated from their original function.

61

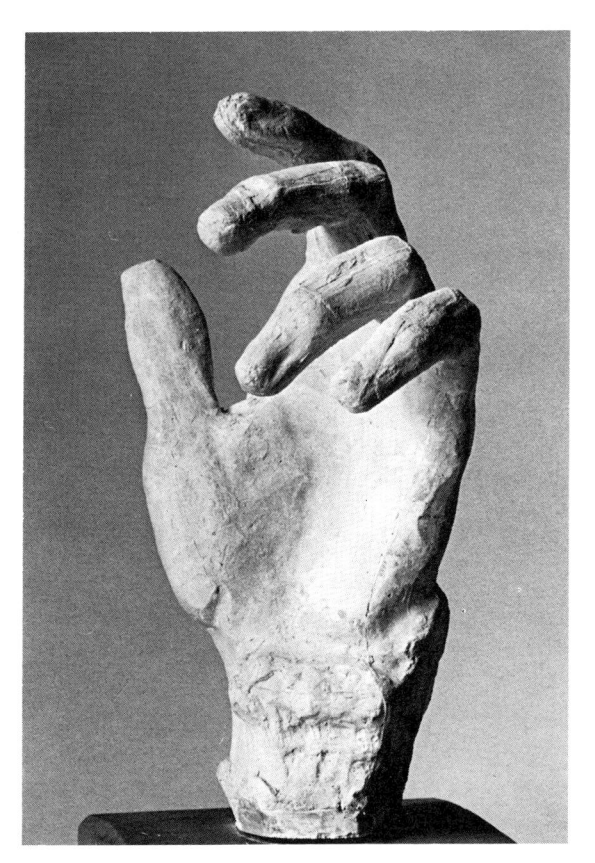

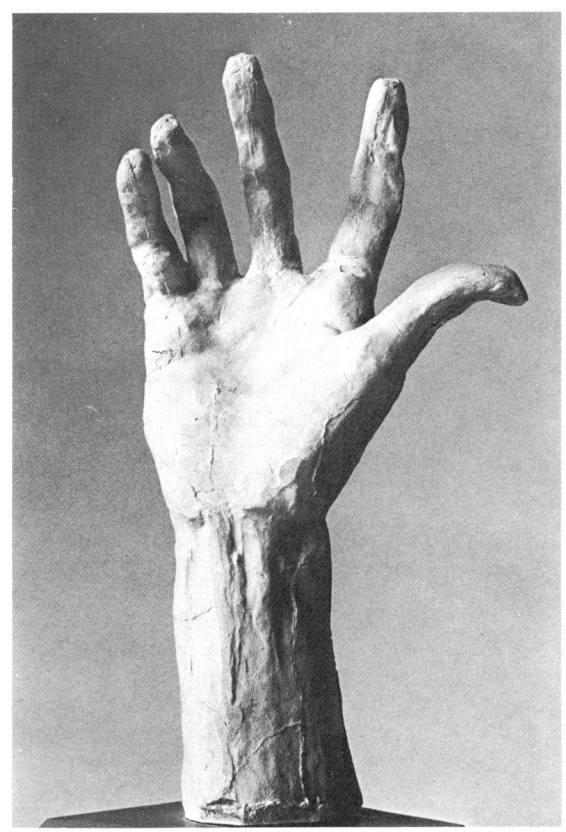

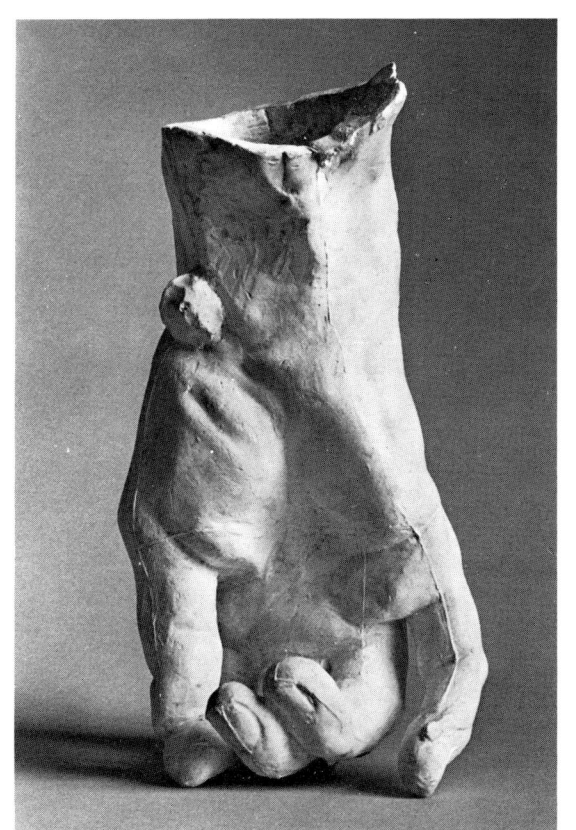

Hands for the figures of the Burghers of Calais, 1886

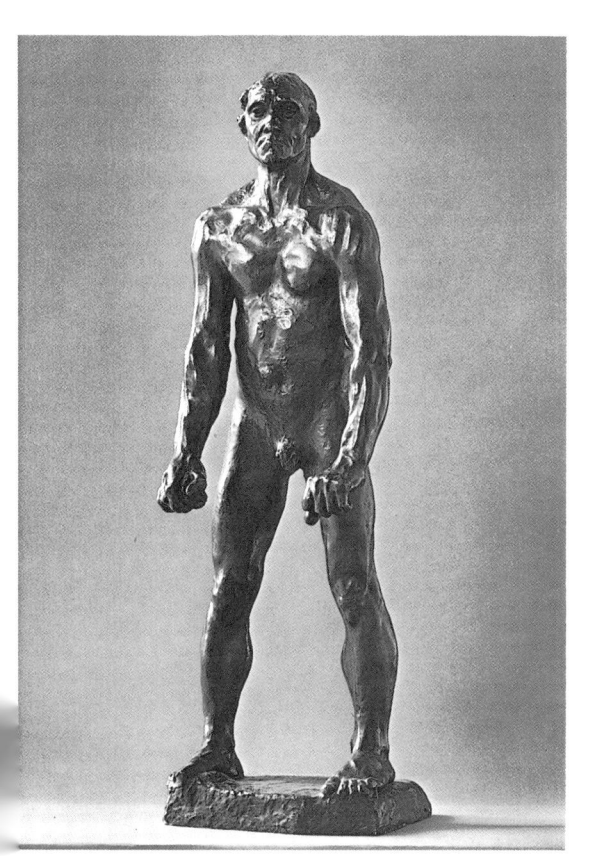

Left: Jean d'Aire, 1886. Right: Eustache de Saint Pierre, 1885

Room 12, general view. In the foreground, By the Sea, towards 190

ROOM 12

Thanks to the large monuments on which he was working and an active policy of international exhibitions, Rodin, on the threshold of the twentieth century at last witnessed the slow and arduous breakthrough of his conceptions of sculpture. In the centre, the plaster cast, *By the Sea,* is a synthesis of several studies of seated bathers and also a reference to the features of the Czech artist, Braunerova, for long time known as "The Slavonic Woman" (see Room 8). Here, in contrast to the restless emotional and dramatic climat of the *Gates of Hell*, Rodin appears to have sought the serenity he so admired in ancient sculpture: "I strive constantly to obtain a calmer view of nature", he confided to the Gustave Coq...

[text obscured by photograph]

...in the relationship between the physical and the spiritual that characterizes the majority of his works. The tense attitude of the *Thinker* gives way here to a far freer position.

In several groups where the titles are very general, the *Good Genius*, the *Bad Genius*, *Exhortation* (1903), the relationship between the figures remains elusive. Timeless, without attributes or accessories, they seem to inhabit a world where gesture has become a means of communication carrying sculptural arrangement to almost choreographic fullness. Another group the *Christ and the Magdalen*, is, along with the *St. John the baptist*, one of Rodin's rare religious sculptures. It portrays a distended, dislocated figure of Christ with a ravaged and bruised countenance and a sinuous Mary Magdalen recalling the shapely body of the *Meditation* belonging to the *Gates of Hell*. This theme has been an iconographical constant since the Middle Ages but the nudity of the two figures accentuates the erotic cha... strangely mingling ... and sensual ecstasy. The ... entitled *Prometheus and Pity*, implying a kind ...tion of Rodin, the ...ator, with the male ... the Magdalen becomes ... muse.

...*npest* (1898), ...ded with plaits ... snakes of some ... the persistence of ... tragic impulse. ...ent titles, such as ... *thon Runner*, ...ing a ... and moral ... be noted that ...ving new names to ...me work was due to a kind of poetic intuition whereby Rodin adhered to an almost literary conception of his art under the influence of symbolism, mutually enriching the forms and the written expression.

By the sea, towards 190

Constellation, 1902

Room 13, general view. In the foreground, Alexandre Falguière, 189

ROOM 13

The distinguished pictures decorating the walls of this room make it a kind of sanctuary of painting amid sculpture. Of the hundred of so which Rodin assembled — acquisitions or presents of very varying interest and quality — the five by Van Gogh, Renoir and Monet shine forth: Van Gogh's portrait of *Old Tanguy* (1887) shows the hardware-dealer of Montmartre against a ground entirely covered with prints of Hokusai and Hiroshige, all perfectly identifiable, a tribute to Van Gogh's love of Japanese art; the *Harvesters* (1888) and the *Blue Train* (1888) with its subtle transpositions of colour belong to Van Gogh's period at Arles; Renoir's *Nude* (1880) is a reminder that he alone of the impressionists used the female figure as a major theme; the canvas by Claude Monet is one of a series of landscapes of Belle-Isle painted in 1886. It bears witness to the bond of friendship linking Monet and Rodin, whose works were shown in a joint exhibition at the Georges Petit gallery in 1889.

Several portraits recall Rodin's connections with the literary, artistic and political circles of the day: the controversial journalist Henri Rochefort, is represented by a bust of 1886 bringing out the caustic and biased personality of the model: the deep-set alert eyes suggest his power of concentration and lively wit and the pronounced facial muscles and rebellious locks of hair sum up his fiery and pugnacious temperament. Aware of the psychological truth of his bust, Rochefort commented: "it is like the synthesis of a whole life which was somewhat eventful. Here, one feels that the model took paths where there were quite a few stones". *Clemenceau*'s portrait was commissioned by the Argentine government to commemorate his series of lectures in South America. The model grew impatient with the eighteen sittings Rodin asked and, being displeased with the result, insisted that the work be shown under an anonymous title because, he said: "Rodin has made me into an oriental, Tamerlane or Gengis Khan". In spite of this criticism, the bust is doubtless one of the freeest and most penetrating portraits of the politician whose enigmatic, contemptuous and determined character is admirably caught by the energetic and animated handling. The painter *Puvis de Chavannes* was also irritated by his portrait. Rodin had transposed into volumes what he liked most in his model, robustness, calm, reserve, without disregarding physical likeness. The type of portrait emerging from a barely-cut block of marble was among those Rodin adopted in opposition to academic canons. There are two examples here. In the one of *Bernard Shaw*, who posed in 1906, Rodin strove to bring out the incisive and bantering features of the irrepressible Irishman who wrote shortly afterwards: "I shall always be proud to be known as your model, you are the only man beside whom I feel really humble". As for the work entitled *Mozart*, it was actually an adaptation of a portrait of the musician Gustav Mahler, whom Rodin defined as "a mixture of Frederick the Great and Mozart", an alliance of will-power and sensibility.

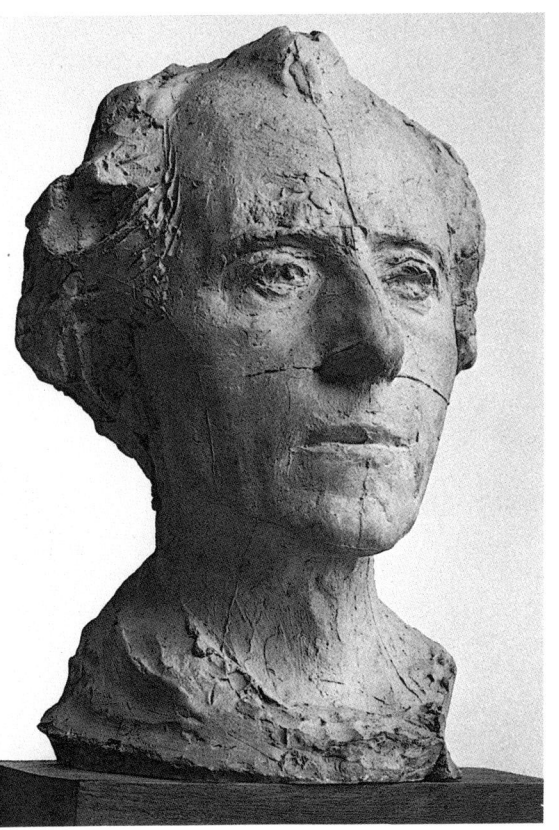

Above: Mozart, 1910. Below: Gustav Malher, 1909 and Georges Clemenceau, 191

Anna de Noailles, 1906

Room 14, general view. In the foreground, study for the monument to Balzac, 189

ROOM 14

The sculptures shown here were designed for various public monuments commissioned from Rodin. Some were left as models but others were completed and erected. Of the first, the group of *Benedictions* recalls a project for a monument to Labour which Rodin had in mind from 1894-1899. It was to be a colossal tower with walls covered in reliefs symbolizing the different human activities and topped by this group of winged genii descending from heaven to bless human toil. Another unrealized project was the statue planned for London in honour of the American painter, Whistler. The few surviving studies of nudes and figures draped in the classical manner to illustrate the subject of the painter's muse are carved in tranquil opulent forms approaching the monumentality of Maillol.

Some of the finished statues were fairly small in size like the monument in Fresselines (Creuse) to the poet Maurice Rollinat. Several sculptures refer to the monument to *Victor Hugo*.

The complicated elaboration of this piece gave rise to a series of models among which Rodin seemed unable to make a clear choice. The monument was to be part of a vast decorative scheme decided in 1885 for the Pantheon. The problem of the poet's physical resemblance had been solved in 1883, the date of a bust in which Rodin minimized the details in order to bring out the most characteristic features, the huge brow and deep-set eyes, symbols of intellectual superiority. After a first series of projects showing Hugo seated on the rock of his exile in Guernsey, Rodin produced the model for the *Apotheosis of Victor Hugo*, in answer to the critics who deemed the former composition muddled. Here, the poet is shown standing and in contemporary dress, a portrayal completed by allegories to exalt the epic quality of the figure. Among these imaginery characters, the compact and harmonious group of Nereids or the *Voice of the Sea* is a repetition of the *Three Sirens* of the *Gates of Hell*.

A number of studies for the statue of *Balzac* studded the slow creation of this work, accepted by some as a manifesto of modern sculpture and by others as a total failure but in any event remaining a provocative achievement of utmost historical and artistic significance. The Société des Gens de Lettres commissioned the work from Rodin in 1891 and he set about his task in the naturalist manner, amassing information concerning the novelist's morphology. The result was an initial series of studies respecting Balzac's physical appearance (he died over 40 years earlier), such as the bust of *Balzac as a Young Man*, taken from a portrait by Deveria, several massive and distorted nudes and the Balzac "robed as a Dominican friar". After interrupting his work from 1892-95, Rodin abandoned the realistic representation of Balzac for a psychological reconstruction, emphasizing his creative genius. This is the argument of the last study before the final monument where Balzac stands in his ageless garment and where the violent and contorted handling of the features, now no longer a portrait, shows that it is the head and not the gesture that makes genius understood.

Nude studies for the monument to Balzac, 1892-1896

Nude study type C for the monument to Balzac, 1892-1893

Bathers, Ornament for a swimming-pool, 190(

ROOM 15

Three different series fill this room: sculptures carved for purely decorative purposes, those devoted to the theme of the hand and those portraying the theme of dance. The first demonstrate that Rodin, even at the height of his fame, had not forgotten that in order to earn his living as a young man and during part of his maturity he had worked as a practitisned on architectural and interior decoration. He consequently never scorned projects of this type, as several pieces show: the *Little Water Sprite* (1890) and the *Woman Fish* (1906) were both designed for a fountain; the originality of the latter lies in the fact that, instead of taking the banal shape of a mermaid with a fish's tail, the aquatic character of the creature is concentrated in the face, its globular eyes, almost non-existent nose and thick round mouth. The *Bacchus at the Vat* (towards 1912) again is a garden sculpture. There is also a project for a fireplace for the South-American art-lover Don Errazuriz, with facings adorned with a somewhat domesticated version of the silhouettes of the Adam and Eve of the *Gates of Hell*. Lastly, the four *Bathers* that decorated the niches of the swimming pool of a mansion in Neuilly, are lithe and pulpy beings who undress, do their hair and rub their limbs with a grace displaying Rodin's sensitivity to the delicate contours and flowing lines of *art nouveau*.

For Rodin, all the parts of the body and the hands especially had an expressive power as great as that of the face, and were capable of conveying personality, ideas, feelings and emotion. The *Hand of the Devil* (1903) to some extent is the sinister answer to the *Hand of God* (see room 4). Another left hand, the *Hand emerging from the Tomb* (1910) takes on threatening significance through its various names (*Punishment* or *Mane, Thecel, Phares*). Technically, it is an example of Rodin's eagerness not to disguise the difficulties linked with the material used: the "bridges" linking the fingers serve to consolidate the form and prevent the parted fingers from breaking. Contrasting with these evil hands, the *Lover's Hands* (before 1909) assemble two right hands, a man's and a woman's, to symbolize their embrace.

For Rodin, the great challenge was how to infuse life into inert matter and to arrest movement. He strove all his life to achieve this but perhaps best demonstrated his purpose in a series of small sculptures devoted to dance. He began these in about 1910, stimulated by the new styles introduced into choreography by Isadora Duncan, Loïe Fuller and the Russian Ballet. "When I was young, seeing our opera ballets, I could not understand what had made the Greeks place dance above all else", he said. Rodin was interested in everything that corresponded to its essence, the lack of convention, the realistic and dynamic aspects of modern dance in the figures called *Dance Movements*. These are free translations of exercizes and the search for balance. Arbitrary distortions of the body such as arms of unequal length or lacking the elbow-bone and muscles emphasized by leaps make them particularly expressive.

Studies of dance movements, towards 191

Nijinsky, 1912

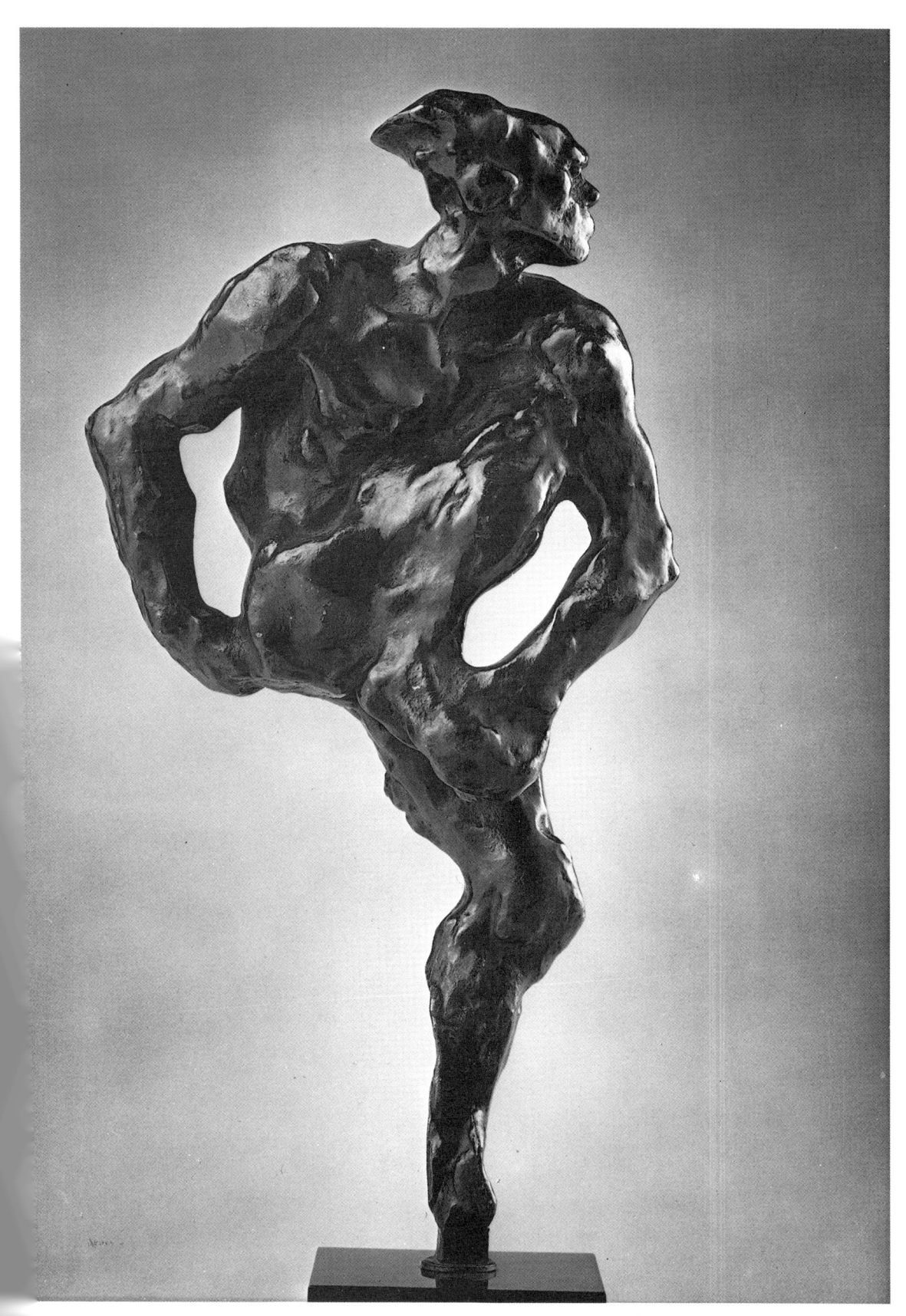

Room 16, general view

ROOM 16

Here, the theme of the couple already encountered in the previous room prevails once more. Making use of titles drawn from mythology, legend or literature, Rodin depicts physical passion with a new freedom, a kind of timeless dignity of the flesh going beyond any hint of licentiousness or anecdote in the embraces portrayed. The *Minotaur* (towards 1886), also called *Jupiter in the form of a Bull* is one of Rodin's many works illustrating Ovid's *Metamorphoses*. Its twin title makes two interpretations possible: that of the lord of the gods in the form of a bull raping Europa, who gave birth to Minos, King of Crete; or that of the monster born of Minos and Pasiphae which, named the Minotaur, each year collected a tribute of seven maidens and seven youths until Theseus put it to death. With its particularly lascivious expression of sensual desire, its life-like but ever elegant forms, the group bears witness to Rodin's fondness of eighteenth-century art acquired during his apprenticeship and the years spent with Carrier-Belleuse. The bull's head reappears in *Pygmalion and Galatea* (1889) showing a satyr or faun personalizing the myth of Pygmalion, the sculptor who fell in love with the statue he had created, brought alive by Aphrodite in response to his beseechings. This too was a mythological theme often treated by eighteenth-century artists; as in the Sèvres biscuit statuette by Falconet, which Rodin no doubt saw while he worked intermittently at the porcelain factory between 1879 and 1882.

Rodin's steady interest in pagan myths naturally inspired the first studies for the *Gates of Hell* between 1880 and 1885. The marble *Psyche-Spring*, also called the *Surprised Nymph* is an example of the separate use Rodin made of one of the subjects originally intended for the reliefs of the *Gates*, to content a private clientèle of art-lovers and collectors. This explains the inward-curving and compact structure chosen in preference to a composition expanding in space' uniting a voluptuous female form and a vibrant male anatomy, the very image of desire.

Of the other groups relating to myths, the *Bacchantes*, the *Nymph's Games*, the majority are the result of the assembly of pre-existing pieces Rodin developed this method owing to the proliferation of the works he had created for the *Gates*, putting the different parts together in sizes and materials often quite unlike the ones originally used and achieving forms that were given new meaning by the change of context. In the *Oceanides*, for instance, the two kneeling figures are based on the *Bacchantes embracing*, but are shown from the back, having lost their cloven feet in their passage from the terrestrial to the marine world. A female figure from the *Gates* bends forward above the couple. Sirens and oceanides were very popular subjects among painters and sculptors at the end of the nineteenth century who incorporated their sinuous outlines and treaming hair in decorative compositions to the taste of *art nouveau*. By beautifying the anatomical details and suppressing the accessories, Rodin has preserved the poetic and imaginative power of the theme.

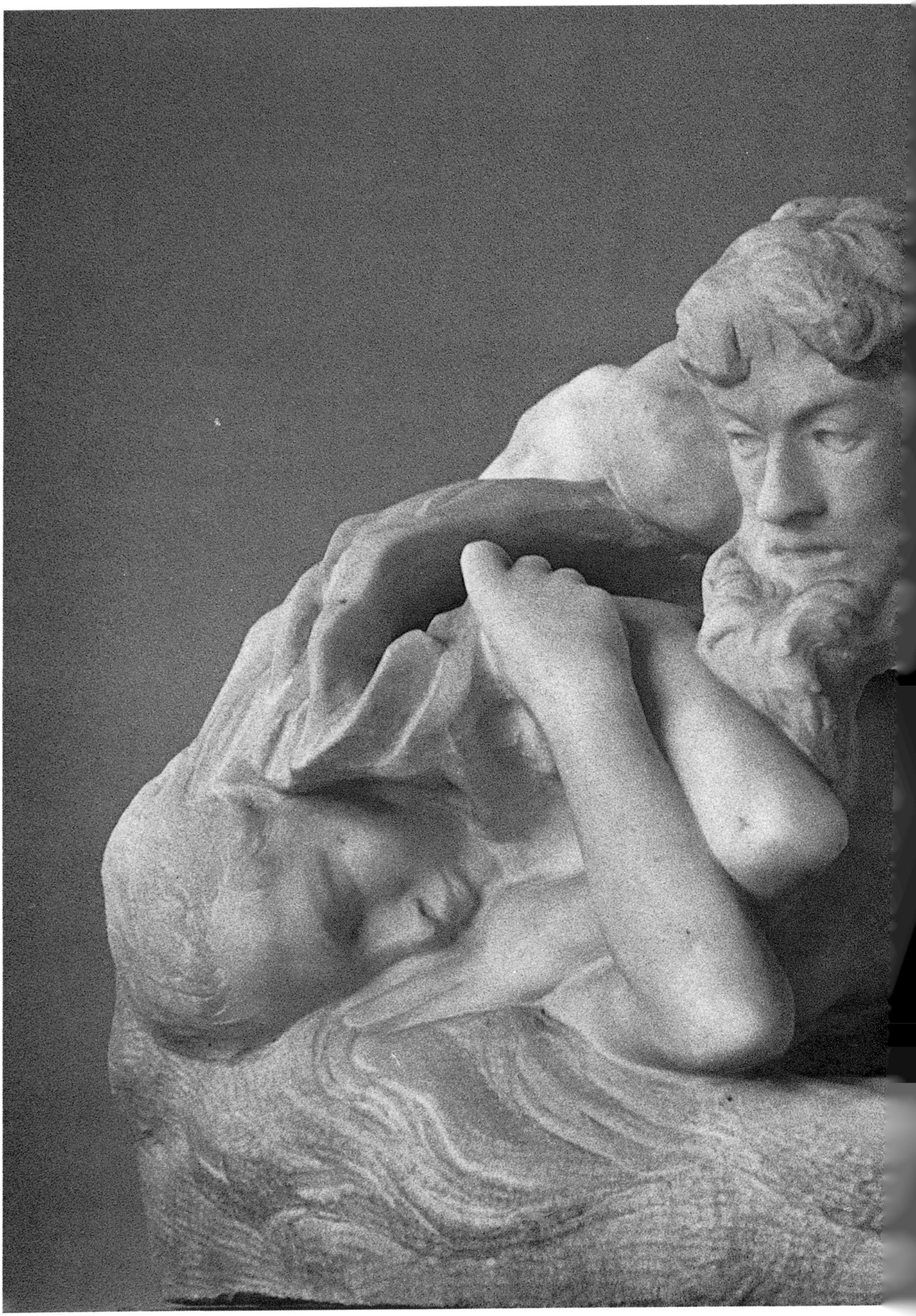

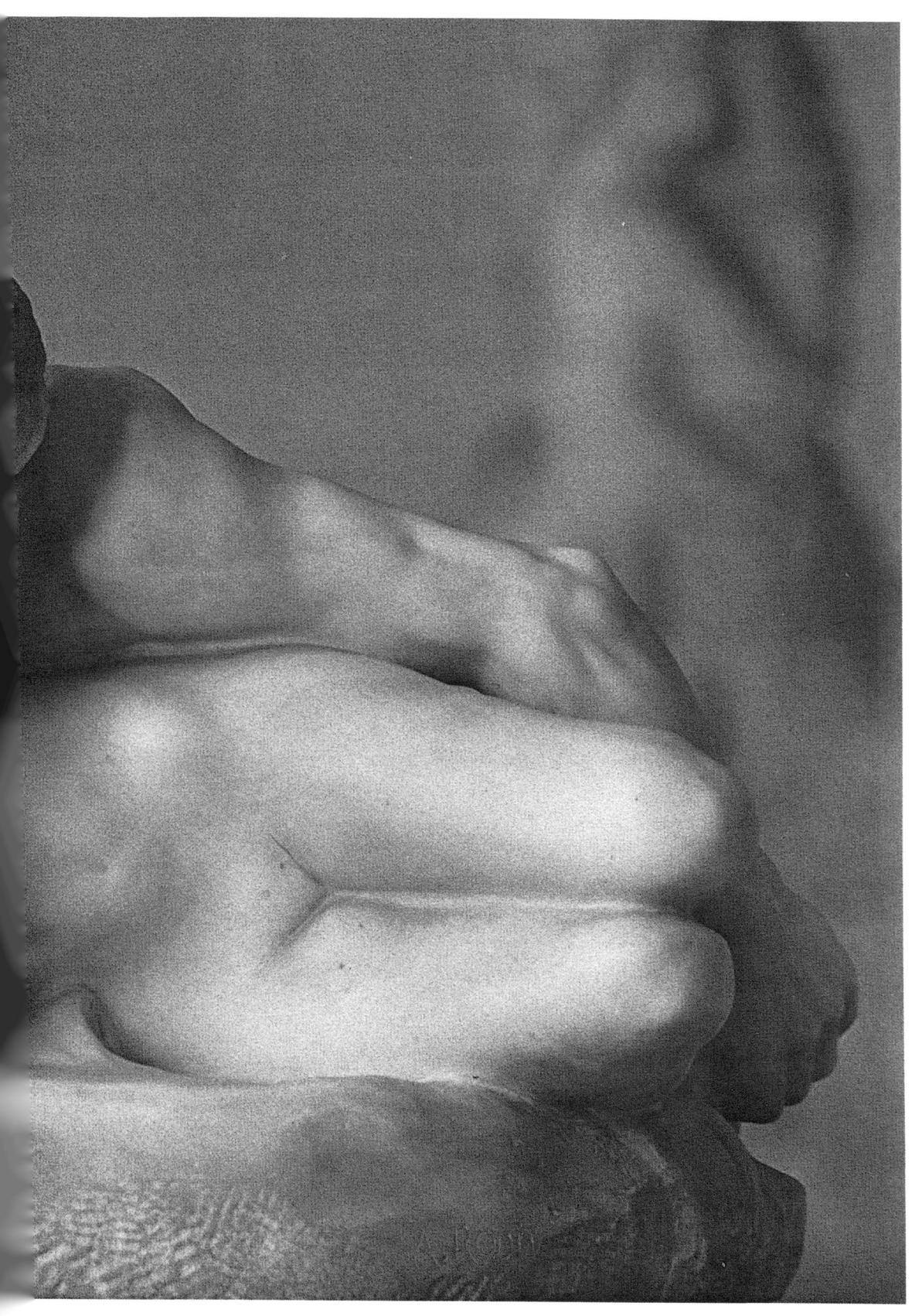

Psyche-Spring, 1885

Balzac, 1891-189[7]

THE GARDENS

The outbuildings for the servants of the household surrounding the forecourt of the Hôtel Biron were altered and enlarged in the nineteenth century for the needs of the Convent of the Sacred Hearth. Of the various chapels that formerly belonged to the community, the vastest, a neo-Gothic structure built from 1875-76 by the architect, Lisch, still borders the rue de Varenne. About fifteen years ago, it was converted into a hall for temporary exhibitions, which might also house an information service, the bookshop and the administration in the event of a restructuration of the museum.

The earlier constructions have been replaced by a rose-garden where the monumental casts of some of the most famous works are shown. On the right, the statue of the *Thinker* looms against the admirable silhouette of the dome built by Jules Hardouin-Mansart for the chapel of Saint-Louis des Invalides. Rodin's most famous work, now so popular that its aesthetic significance almost seems overlooked, is the focal point and central figure of the *Gates of Hell* (see room 9). Its success made Rodin decide to produce an enlargement by a mechanical technique derived from the pantograph. His assistant, Lebossé, in charge of the operation, wrote in 1903: "Far from losing by the enlargement, your sculpture has gained in grandeur and truth to life while preserving your personal touch". Owing to its reputation the *Thinker* has gradually become a public symbol, forfeiting its special iconographical meaning to join the sparse ranks of well-loved basic works. The first enlarged cast was financed by public subscription and was erected in front of the Panthéon in 1906. It was transferred to the garden of the museum in 1922.
A little to the right of the house stands the statue of *Balzac*. The plaster model shown at the 1898 Salon had aroused adverse reactions from a public disconcerted by this rendering of a celebrated figure where physical likeness and respect of reality were non-existent.

The Gates of hell was commissioned by the State in 1880 and Rodin was to work at it for the rest of his life, with long periods of interruption when he turned to other tasks. It was not in his nature to finish one sculpture before starting another; on the contrary, it seemed as if tackling several projects simultaneously stimulated and enriched his imagination. Directing the mounting of the figures and groups designed for the *Gates* (see Rooms 9 and 10) on the plaster support set up in his workshop was to be one of his last undertakings. He was never to see it in bronze, as the five versions now existing (one in Paris, two in the United States, one in Switzerland, one in Japan) were cast posthumously.
In the first models, Rodin had in mind the bronze doors of the Italian Renaissance, especially Ghiberti's *Gates of Paradise* at the Baptistry in Florence with their strictly symmetrical panels divided into squares covered with storied reliefs and framed with decorative foliage. But his desire to achieve a personal rendering led him to choose more luxuriant ornamentation, spilling out of the architectural frame, animated by turbulent forms and

light and shade effects. These were all features closely attuned to the aesthetics of *art nouveau* at the turn of the century, propagated throughout Europe by art magazines and by exhibitions in which Rodin participated.

The subject-matter, is the torments of Hell, but treated in a symbolist and non narrative fashion. The lintel dominating the doors offers an amazing piece of carving with three thicknesses of superimposed figures treated in sharp relief as they are intended to be viewed from a distance (the *Gates* are 6.35 metres high). Confined by the powerful moulding, the gesticulation of these figures is in fact highly organized in a sweeping movement from left to right marked by a woman, shown several times against the crowd behind her.

In his attempt to achieve a generalisation, a visionary portrayal of genius, Rodin totally rejected the standards of his time. These consisted in illustrating famous men by meaningful gestures and showing them in recognizable attitudes and contemporary dress. Rodin himself had followed them in the monuments to *Claude Lorrain* and *Victor Hugo*. Here, laying the accent on inner life, Rodin endowed his figure with a proud stance suggesting the superiority of a great man. The light unifies the mounting lines of the robe leading to the inordinately tormented face, the expression of the soul of a genius. A menhir, a cube, Rodin's *Balzac* is at the source of the sculpture of our century.

To the left of the forecourt, the group depicting the *Burghers of Calais* is one of the ten versions found in different parts of the world, cast from the model kept in the museum. The first was unveiled in Calais in 1895. When compared with the preparatory studies (see room 11), the monumental version stresses the tragic character of the figures by the hollowing out of the eyes and the wrinkles and the complex articulation of the clothing. The presentation without a pedestal, "very low to allow the public to sense the spirit of the subject" (Rodin to the Mayor of Calais) adds to the idea of sacrifice. The hostages are no longer deified like supernatural heroes, they are intended to reach the inner recesses of citizen's hearts.

Behind the Hôtel lies the garden proper. On the terrace running along the south front, two large *Caryatids* face each other. These figures are enlargements of a subject designed for the *Gates of Hell*, in which Rodin entirely renewed the old theme of the bearer figure. Greek art portrayed the Caryatid as impassive and serene but here, her form crushed beneath her burden, she expresses the sorrows laden on mankind. The functional character of the statue is effaced by its psychological signifiance.

The other bronzes further down the garden: *Ugolino, Eve, Meditation, The Call to Arms,* are likewise Rodin's own enlargements of works exhibited inside the museum in their original size.

The space is filled with tumbling forms, among which a skeleton recalls the morbid atmosphere of medieval *danses macabres* illustrating the chaos, destruction and terror of death as well as the allegorical theme of its equalizing might. The two panels are bordered by lateral pilasters, carved in softer relief. The curved, contorted shapes seem to be suffocating within the moulded frame that grips them, creating a feeling of constraint and

The Burghers of Calais, 1886

The Burghers of Calais, details

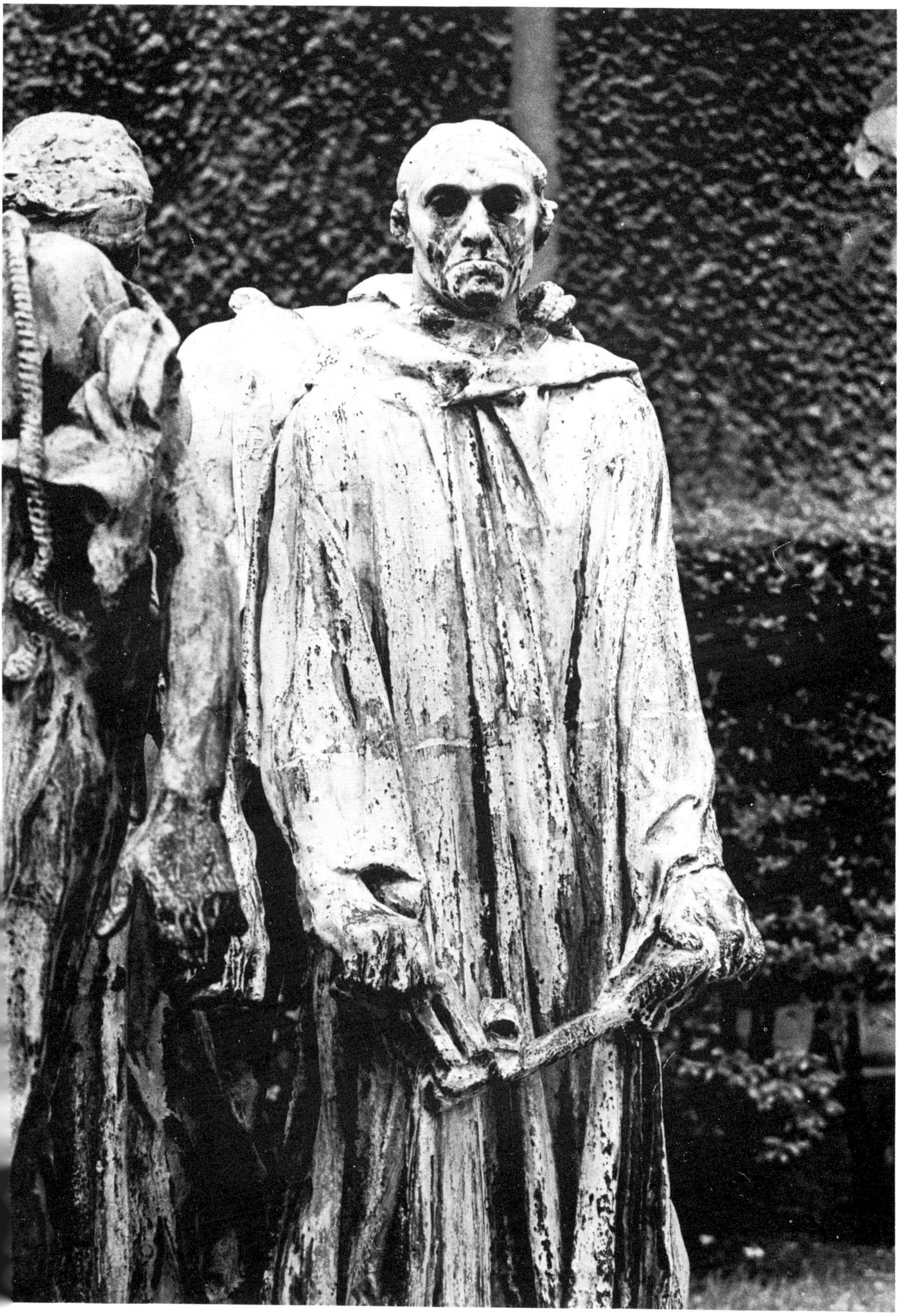

suffering, eloquently expressing "the accursed lovers ever entwined and never appeased..." (Octave Mirbeau). The surfaces of the panels swarm with about 150 characters joined by movements of a daring and freedom unknown hitherto. Rodin expended enormous energy on this assignment, finding himself obliged to think in terms of a monumental composition on a gigantic scale, owing to the breadth of his conception, and to give his art a philosophical scope rarely tackled in nineteenth-century sculpture. This led him to use a type of structure which upset all the canons of the narrative tradition; the figures intermingle in a very ambiguous sculptural area full of unevennesses where the volumes alter with the changing light. The *Gates of Hell* had no precedent and no real following; it is *fin-de-siècle* by the pessimistic sensibility it reflects but far in advance of its time by its formal audacity. It is a work that fascinates, disconcerts, disturbs and the presence of the two large figures of *Adam* and *Eve* on either side, placed there to call up original sin, add a further interrogation to the pathos and violence of its universe.

The Gates of Hell, 1880-1917

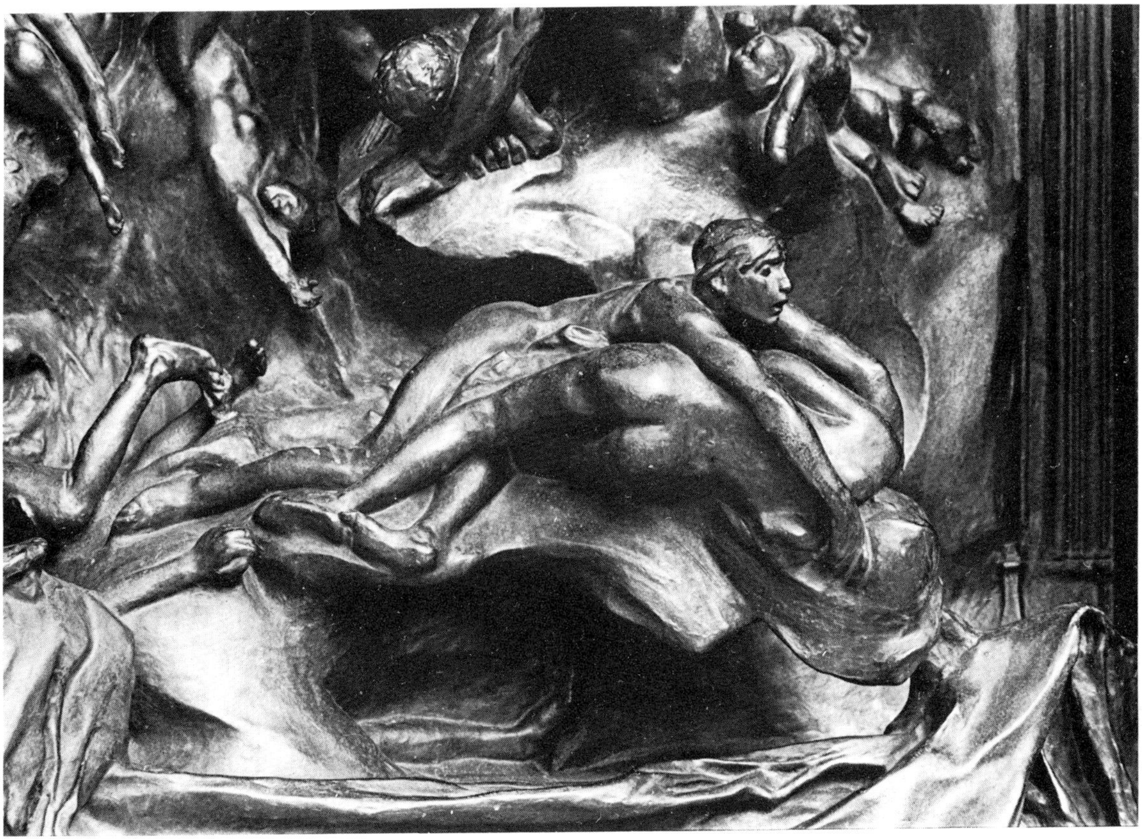

The Gates of Hell, details

Rodin in his studio

CHRONOLOGY

1840
Birth of François Ausguste René Rodin on 12 November in Paris. His father, Jean-Baptiste Rodin, was a modest civil servant from Normandy and his mother, Marie Cheffer, a farmer's daughter from the east of the france. Rodin went to the local school, soon demonstrating a love of drawing.

1851-54
Attended a boarding-school in Beauvais where his uncle was headmaster. Mediocre studies.

1854-58
Rodin's vocation for drawing made his father decide to register him at the School of Decorative Arts (known as the Petite Ecole). There he followed the excellent courses given by Horace Lecoq de Boisbaudran. In addition to drawing, Rodin also learned modelling and began to visit the Louvre and the Gallery of Prints and Engravings at the National Library. He studied animal anatomy at the Jardin des Plantes, where the animal sculptor, Barye, sometimes supervised his work; he also followed courses in drawing from the model at the Gobelins National Tapestry Factory.
He failed the competitive entrance examination to the School of Fine Arts (the Grande Ecole) three times.

1860-61
Unable to continue being supported by his parents, Rodin began work as an ornamentist and moulder for the decoration of many houses being built in Paris at that time, striking up a friendship with the sculptor Dalou. His carving of his father's bust, *Jean-Baptiste Rodin*, is his earliest work preserved. At the death of his elder sister, Maria, Rodin experienced a religious crisis and entered the order of the Very Blessed Sacrament as a novice, but the Reverend Eymard who posed for urged him to pursue his vocation as a sculptor.

1864
Still working as a decorator for a livelihood, Rodin carved the *Man with the Broken Nose*, which was rejected by the Salon des Artistes français. He met Rose Beuret, who remained his life-long companion, and was finally engaged as a modeller in the workshop of Carrier-Belleuse, one of the most fashionable sculptors of the Second Empire.

1866
Birth of his son, Auguste Beuret.

1870-71
With the outbreak of the Franco-Prussian War, Rodin was recruited in the National Guard but was soon discharged on account of his shortsightedness. After the armistice he followed Carrier-Belleuse to Belgium, working on the decoration of several public buildings under his guidance in particular the Stock Exchange in Brussels.

1873
Having broken with Carrier-Belleuse he joined the sculptor Joseph Van Rasbourg as a partner for the execution of ornamental assignments: the Palais des Arts in Brussels, a monument to the Burgomaster, Loos, in Antwerp, etc.

1875-76
Visited Italy (Turin, Genoa, Pisa, Florence, Rome) where he was profoundly impressed by Michelangelo.

1877
The *Age of Bronze*, Rodin's first great personal work, was shown first in Brussels and then in Paris. He was suspected of having cast it on the living model. On his return to Paris, he began work on the *Walking Man* and the *St. John the Baptist*.

1878-79
Carried out various decorative assignments in the south of France, particularly in Nice.

1879
After their reconciliation, Carrier-Belleuse found employment for Rodin at the Sèvres National Porcelain Factory of which he was the director. Rodin worked there for three years; designing ornamental motifs for the decoration of vases.

1880
The *Age of Bronze*, in bronze, was purchased by the State. Rodin was commissioned to carve a monumental door for the Museum of Decorative Arts in Paris, the *Gates of Hell*, at which he was to work for the rest of his life.

1881-82
Unsuccessful in the competition for the monument to Lazare Carnot. Invited to London by his friend Alphonse Legros who introduced him to engraving. Obtained a workshop at the National Marbles Depôt, 182, rue de l'Université. Among his pupils was Camille Claudel, who was to become his assistant, his model and his mistress.

1884
Won the competition for the statue of the French seventeenth-century painter, *Claude Lorrain*, in Nancy. In November, showed the first model for the *Burghers of Calais*.

1885
Signed a contract for the *Burghers of Calais*. Received a commission for a statue of the painter Bastien-Lepage in Damvilliers, in the east of France.

1886
State commission for the great marble, the *Kiss*.

1888
Made Knight of the Legion of Honour.

1889
Joint exhibition with the impressionist painter, Claude Monet. Received a commission for a monument to *Victor Hugo* for the Pantheon in Paris. However, as Rodin neglected the recommendations given, the work was refused. The result was a version in marble, showing the seated nude, which was placed in the gardens of the Palais Royal in Paris in 1909 and is now in the Rodin Museum in Meudon.

1890-91
Took up residence in Meudon-Bellevue, in the southern suburbs of Paris. The Société des Gens de Lettres commissioned him to carve a statue of *Balzac*.

1892
Received a second commission for a monument to *Victor Hugo*, shown standing, for the Pantheon. This was never finished.

1893
Rodin was elected President of the sculpture section of the National Fine Arts Society of which he was a founder.

1894
Worked at a project for the *Tower of Labour*, not executed.

1895
Purchased the Villa des Brillants in Meudon. Worked at the monument to *Sarmiento*, the Argentine hero (Apollo slaying the Python). The *Burghers of Calais* was unveiled in the Place Richelieu in Calais.

1897
Publication of an extensive study of Rodin's drawings with a preface by Octave Mirbeau.

1898
The Salon of the National Fine Arts Society showed the plaster cast of the monument to *Balzac*. Conflict with the members of the Société des Gens de Lettres who regarded the work as unfinished; violent press campaign. Break with Camille Claudel.

1899
The Balzac affair added to Rodin's notoriety. Triumphal journey to Belgium and Holland. Rodin began the statue of the painter Puvis de Chavannes, which remained unfinished but of which there is a marble bust and a marble figure called the *Genius of Eternal Rest*.

1900-01
In the context of the Exposition Universelle in Paris, Rodin organized the first vast retrospective of his work; 170 sculptures and drawings were shown in a pavilion specially built for the purpose in the Place de l'Alma. His international reputation benefited greatly as a result. He enlarged his workshop, welcoming Bourdelle, Despiau, the Schegg brothers, Pompon, Desbois, and founded a school of sculpture, the Rodin Academy, in Paris. The American photographer Edward Steichen, photographed Rodin's sculptures at Meudon.

1902
Began to correspond with the poet, Rainer Maria Rilke. Triumphal visit to London.

1903
On the death of the painter, Whistler, became President of the International Society of Sculptors, Painters and Engravers. Worked on the monument to *Whistler*, which was never finished.

1905
Liaison with the Duchess of Choiseul, his "Muse", which led to conflicts with some longstanding friends. A large model of the *Thinker*, cast in bronze thanks to a public subscription was erected in front of the Pantheon in Paris (removed to the gardens of the Rodin Museum in 1922. In October the poet, Rainer Maria Rilke became Rodin's secretary. Rodin made Doctor Honoris Causa of the University of Jena.

1906
Sketched the Cambodian dancing-girl who accompanied King Sisowath on his visit to France, in Meudon and Marseille. Visited Spain with the painter, Zuloaga. Dismissed Rilke: owing to the latter's patient and admiring understanding, the two were reconciled later. Made Doctor Honoris Causa of the University of Glasgow.

1907
Made Doctor Honoris Causa of the University of Oxford.

1908
Rilke drew Rodin's attention to the beauty of the Hôtel Biron, an eighteenth-century house in the aristocratic quarter of Paris, the Faubourg Saint-Germain; he moved there in order to entertain and work each afternoon but continued to live in Meudon.

1910
Made Grand Officier of the Legion of Honour.

1911-12
Break with the Duchess of Choiseul. Travelled to London to discuss the site for the group of the *Burghers of Calais* purchased by the British Government that year. Press campaign for the founding of a Rodin Museum. The project won the support of artists, writers and politicians.

1914
At the outbreak of the First World War, Rodin and Rose Beuret went to England. Judith Cladel, Rodin's biographer organized the visit and accompanied them. On their return, they stayed in the south of France. Rodin's health deteriorated.

1915
Travelled to Italy where he began a portrait of Pope Benedict XV.

1916
After impassioned discussions, the State accepted Rodin's donation of the whole of his works, including reproduction rights, and his personal collections.

1917
On 29 January, Rodin married Rose Beuret, who died on 16 February. Rodin died on 17 November and was buried on 24 November beside Rose in the garden of the Villa des Brillants in Meudon; the statue of the *Thinker* watches over the grave.